The Idea of
Being Indians
and the
Making of India

The Idea of Being Indians and the Making of India

ACCORDING TO THE MISSION STATEMENTS
OF THE REPUBLIC OF INDIA,
AS ENLISTED IN THE PREAMBLE TO THE
CONSTITUTION OF INDIA

George Varuggheese

PARTRIDGE
A Penguin Company

Partridge books may be ordered through booksellers or by contacting:

Partridge India
Penguin Books India Pvt.Ltd
11, Community Centre, Panchsheel Park, New Delhi 110017
India
www.partridgepublishing.com
Phone: 000.800.10062.62

Contents

Preface

To the Citizens of India that is Bharat

This is a book written to inform my fellow citizens of India, that is Bharat, that the idea of being Indians and the idea of the making of India have to be sought in the Constitution of India. Because, Constitution of India was written as the blue print for building the India of the dreams held by 'we the people' of the Independent India, a dream that was nurtured and nourished by the spiritual and cultural history of Bharat. Though the Constitution of India is generally perceived as a book of laws and regulations, it is fundamentally a book enshrining the Mission Statements of the Republic of India and details to attain those missions.

The Preamble to the Constitution of India contains the conceptual design for a resurgent and resplendent India, visualized and recorded by the founding fathers in the

Constituent Assembly on our behalf, as representatives of, 'we
the people' of India. It contains the Mission Statements of
the Republic of India. The 395 Articles of the Constitution
of India, divided into 22 Parts and the Schedules appended
to them are the detailed design frame work developed on the
basis of the conceptual design in the Preamble.

The conceptual design in the Preamble is based on the 'total
system or holistic approach' originally found in the Scriptures
belonging to India or Bharat. This is a natural phenomenon
in that throughout the history of human society, we could
see that constitution making and nation building activities
had drawn inspirations from Scriptures which were followed
by the individuals or groups who were instrumental in such
constitution making and nation building activities.

If we look at the Preamble to the Constitution of India as
the Mission Statements of the Republic of India for the
welfare of the people at 100% population level and then look
at today's Indian society, we find wide and frightening gap
between the missions set forth in the Constitution of India
and their realization at physical, mental and social level of
our society. The reason for this is because, the Constitution
was not used as a design aid to create a conceptual framework
in the minds of people at total level of the population as to
what role they had to play and what they should expect from
their government in the making of the Indians as well as the
India envisioned in the Constitution of India.

The idea of being Indians and making of the India of that
idea, is essentially creative works of Indians. Indians, the
people of Bharat, should be identified as people who are
trying to climb the divine heights of health, prosperity and

peace through the attainments of the missions set forth in the Constitution of India. But, existing cultural environment and social structures need to be remodeled and rebuilt for that great task because, on India's emergence from a colonial state to a republican state, we failed to remodel and restructure the administrative, judicial and police systems specifically created by the colonial government for executing its goals of revenue maximization by subjugating and oppressing the people of India.

This book is an effort to explore why we as a society and our national and regional governments failed to create the cultural environment and social structure required for a genuinely true democratic republic in the post-independence India and how we can rectify that failure.

For rectification, two major steps are advocated for 'we the people' of India to take. One, expand the scope of 'right to life' to cover the rights to shelter, food, healthcare, education, living wage and social harmony. For, without these, the right to life assured in the Constitution is meaningless. Two, the administrative, judicial and police systems inherited from the feudal British colonizers, should be changed to a *sarvodaya* development model of administrative, judicial and police systems.

Why the egalitarian and holistic welfare goals of a republican state enunciated in the Preamble was not whole-heartedly translated in the lengthy, verbal marathon of Articles of the Constitution and instead of dismantling and discarding the British made feudal governance systems, they were thrust upon the newly emergent democratic India, are mysteries needing focused investigation and intelligent debate among the intellectuals of not only of India but the whole world.

We have a clue for this mystery, in the writings of Jawaharlal Nehru. In his book, *The Discovery of India,* he had stated that the Indian middle class leaders who fought for freedom of India wanted only the British to go and not their 'crushing' ruling systems and structures! These 'crushing' systems and structures which the British used to rule over Indians, were to be used by Indian middle class leaders in the independent India, according to Nehru.

It is a huge misfortune of Indians that the middle class leaders and the political parties they control and share power in ruling the states and the federal nation, are still wallowing in the filth of feudal fascist manipulative power churned out by the 'crushing' systems and structures shaped by the British rulers. It is a misfortune of indescribable magnitude again that almost all institutions of education, healthcare, mass media, bureaucracy, judiciary, police and business corporates are controlled by the middle class owing allegiance and admiration to the legacy left by British rulers. Looking at the behavior of our political class and civil society in not questioning and demanding the replacement of the revenue model of governance structures established by the British colonial rulers, with republican development model of governance structures, one wonders whether the majority of Indians understand what democratic republican society is and its role in the development of human personality!

A look at the structure of governments in states and at federal level will convince us that revenue maximization is being given precedence over socio-economic development. The conflict between revenue maximization and development had taken a portent turn in 2012, with the case of wireless spectrum allocation when welfare oriented decision of telecommunication ministry was shot down by the supreme court in favor of revenue maximization advocated by the finance ministry and its auditing wing. Surprisingly and sadly, larger section of public also seemed to favor the revenue maximization stand of the auditing wing of the government.

If the feudal British colonial government in India treated Indians like vassals, as Nehru had written in *The Discovery of India,* then the Republican India's government also had not made much improvement in treating its masters, the people of India! The labor which is the only asset of a vast section of poor people is still valued at as low or as high price as was accorded by feudal lords to their vassals.

Instead of raising the value of labor of the people uniformly at 100% population level, giving pittance in the name of inclusivity to the vast section of the Indian population, is again the vestige of feudal mind unwilling to retreat to its place in the history. What persuaded the republican India's government to fix not only living wages but a grand luxury scale wages to its employees while closing its eyes to the pitiable penurious conditions of the majority of the working forces in the country? Was it not obligatory on its part to give equal opportunity, status and compensation to all working population without any discrimination, according to the Mission Statements of the Indian Republic, as listed in the Preamble to the Constitution of India?

It is a shame that 80% of the revenue collected by Indian states and the federal government is spent on the government staff and while the remaining 20% is allocated for development projects, a major part of it goes to the middlemen in both government and private sectors.

Gandhiji wanted a uniform wage pattern for all white collar and blue collar work forces, including the menial workers and craftsmen, as the living needs of people across all classes were almost same. The apostle of non-violence had always maintained that keeping the workers without proper wages was also a kind of violence which slowly led people to starve and die untimely.

According to Dr. Amartya Sen, only 20% of the Indians are well off economically and in all respects of comfortable living. It is this section that strives to take India into the super power club while 80% of their fellowmen and women struggle to survive. With these two Indias before us, our idea of being Indians is indeed blurred. But at the same time, we have a hope for having a *Ramarajya* at some time, sooner than later, because of the Mission Statements of the Republic before us, in the form of the Preamble to the Constitution of India. These Mission Statements are capable of being translated into health, prosperity and peace at 100% population level and that is the idea of being Indians and the making of India with that idea—Indians of health, prosperity and peace at 100% population level.

But why this phenomenon of two Indias of vast disparity in standard of living? Is it not the sign that Indian society is still feudal in mental make-up and transactions both inwardly and outwardly? It means, the revolution that got freedom for India from Britons was not a revolution that was necessitated by the moral superiority of an evolved mental state of a society! It was, as Nehru diagnosed, the result of selfish desire of the Indian middle class leaders to take over control of government in the name of self-government and rule India with the same government structures which were created and nurtured by the British colonial government to exploit Indians and send revenue back to England. It is self evident now that they wrote the noble texts of the Preamble to the Constitution of India, with good intention but without any noble desire to fulfill them with their own hands.

Just as the people who wrote Chandogya Upanishad and Mundaka Upanishad in which we have the *'mahavakyas'* such as *'tat tvam asi'* and *'satyam eva jayate'* cannot be held guilty of not achieving what they preached, the people who wrote the noble missions of the Preamble to the Constitution of India cannot be accused of not following what they preached. It was easy for them to copy from the Declaration of American Independence whose writers depended on the scriptural verity that the Creator and the created worlds and people were not two separate entities but one and the same creative force, as the self evident truth to direct the conduct of the American people as free democratic republican nation.

But, one question still remains pertinent and that is: Why Nehru who diagnosed the major fault line of the Indian middle class leadership as its ardent feudalistic pursuit of power and pelf, became helpless in tackling that fault line? What do we do, as that fault line still continues to intimidate the Indian nation?

Mahatma Gandhi, who tried to reform the Indian middle class of its fascist-feudal mind, with *sarvodaya* oriented socio-economic programs through the political parties, especially Congress, the leading national party, was isolated by all of them as they felt threatened for survival. If *sarvodaya* was made the goal for parties, then, there would be need for only workers and not for *netas* and likewise need for parties also would have come down to one or two parties. Not fourteen hundred, as that was the figure for the number of parties registered with the Election Commission of India as of December 2012. We are heading towards a farcical stage in the political history of our nation where, we will have hundreds of political parties to share power in coalition governments. But, the fact is that, the Mission Statements of the Indian republic contained in the Preamble to the Constitution of India is *sarvodaya* in character and their fulfillment entails consensual efforts from all political parties.

When *sarvodya* i.e. rise of people at 100% population level is the goal of the Indian Republic, having 1400 political parties vying to deliver that goal is a bit farcical if not outlandish and primitive competition for selfish gains of power and pelf!

The idea of being Indians and the making of India according to the Mission Statements of the Indian Republic as contained in the Preamble to the Constitution of India is about making Indians healthy, prosperous and peaceful at 100% population level using the *sarvodaya* concept in governance. While a 12-point *sarvodaya* model of good governance is presented in the book, its implementation is envisaged at all municipal and *panchayat* wards level in India. This model is applicable world-wide.

The book has no list of references appended at the end as relevant hints are given in the texts itself. In this age of Internet, readers are able to access to all alluded sources of information. Moreover, eternal verities are impervious to human scholarship and intellectual critique and eternal verities govern the supreme actions, the people of India had decided to undertake for themselves as a republic and recorded them in the Preamble to the Constitution of India, as missions of the Indian Republic. The Oneness of the Creator and the created men and women, the inherent oneness among the members of the human race and the Law of Evolution controlling the progress or perdition of the human race, are the eternal verities that govern the missions of the Republic of India. Democracy, equality, liberty and fraternity are conditions facilitating human evolution forward for successful living. Justice is the fulfillment of these conditions for the sovereign, autonomous evolution of every single member of the human race, apportioned and appropriated by different nation states of the world.

Tat tvam asi, advaita, aham brahmasmi etc are concepts equivalent to the Biblical concept of men and women being *godimages(images of God)*. The founding fathers of American Republic had used this concept of *godimages* as the self evident truth that demanded democratic and republican governance for happy and successful living. That was the reason for their taking their oath of allegiance in the name of the Holy Bible. A majority of leaders who signed the Declaration of American Independence were Free Masons and Rosicrucian adherents who believed in the oneness of God and His creation, like the Hindus believed. A true democrat is a lover of the humankind as a whole, starting with his or her family, neighborhood, state and nation. He or she likes to do to others what he or she wants others do for him or her. The idea of being Indians is to have a system approach to life where every Indian is a sovereign member of the Indian Republic, which on its part is a sub-system in the world of nations on Earth, while Earth itself is a part of the cosmos, the whole system. Of course, the individual Indian is simultaneously part of various sub-systems such as the family, local community, religions, political parties, state etc. which are aids to the attainment of the objectives of the Indian Republic, as enlisted in the Preamble to the Constitution of India.

Many years ago when Francis Bacon who was the Imperator or the Grand Master of the Rosicrucian Society of England gave leadership to colonize America, he had visualized a New Atlantis of ideal democratic society, rising out of the American Continent. In the lost Continent of Atlantis, such a society existed according to the records available with the monastic communities across the world.

According to the legends circulating among world societies and records available with various monasteries in the East and West, there existed a Continent named Atlantis and that Continent went under the waters of the Atlantic Ocean, 12000 years ago. Sinking of Atlantis had started some 80,000 years ago and according to the monastic records which was accessible to Francis Bacon as head of the mystical organization known as the Rosicrucian Society of England, today's three major civilizations i.e. the Aryan, the Egyptian and the Mexican, had been nurtured by the people who escaped from Atlantis before it perished. With his mystical power, he could visualize a world order rising from the land of America with people from all parts of the world settling there and establishing a model democratic republic, a forerunner to the new world order of universal brotherhood fated for the inhabitants of Earth. Believe it or not, today who emigrate to America are those from these three civilizations and many of them had lived in the lost Continent of Atlantis in their previous births, according to Rosicrucian and Theosophical literature available to the public at large.

The Preamble to the Constitution of India is, as mentioned earlier, a *sarvodaya* model for good governance on the basis of *advaita* or *godimages* concept. A true *Ramarajya* can be built by Indians with the help of this *sarvodaya* model contained in the Preamble to the Constitution of India.

As Nehru indicated in his book, *The Discovery of India,* before the British came to colonize India, we were one of the most prosperous among world nations. India also had village level self governing and self sufficient socio-economic-political systems which were the envy of other nations. Today, we are one of the poorest nations with UNDP's human development index (HDI) ranking at 136 in 2013. It was 134 in 2011. We can change this if we want. We could still be in the fore front of nations as we used to be before the advent of the crude, feudal and bad section of the middle class of England who allied with the bad section of the Indian middle class to give birth to the 'great Indian middle class' which sent back the British but retained their 'crushing structure', to run the republican India, as Nehru had predicted in The Discovery of India.

We have to change the 'crushing structure' which we had retained from the British. We have to create new republican, people-development structures instead of the feudal revenue collection oriented government structure which exists for itself. Are you willing? If yes, let us start from our village and municipality wards. Let us build the India of our dreams through the village and urban wards.

We need an India Development Service instead of IAS which was organized on the model of former ICS under British rule. The IDS personnel should work from every local government ward in urban and village areas implementing the Mission Statements of the Indian Republic as contained in the Preamble to the Constitution of India. We need the judicial system to work on the fraternal conflict resolution model working from every village and municipal wards to suit the republican goals listed in the Preamble to the Constitution. We need police force to support the fraternal conflict resolution system of the village and municipal wards. We need police force filled with 50% women and the minimum education level of police should be graduates with sociological and psychological specialization.

We need neighborhood schools, colleges, nursing homes and hospitals in every wards of the urban and village governments. We need family as the focus of development. We need family as the training and education center of good citizenship. We need family as the character building platform on which the national and world civilizational moorings for universal brotherhood will depend.

We need equality between sexes, castes, religions and regions nurtured at homes. We need health, education, houses, food, income security and social harmony at 100% population level. All these are assured by the Mission Statements of our Republic as listed in the Preamble to the Constitution of India. These missions of the Indian Republic have to be taught to the children of India through their parents at home If we have career, status, wealth and fame but do not have credit of having brought up a good citizen, as parents, then we have earned really nothing in the life we had got to live on earth!

We should have done all these right from the day we became a free nation in 1947. Why we could not do so has been narrated in the four chapters of this book. What we have to do to make up our lapse also is given in the book. Yes, the idea of being Indians and the idea of the making of India, that we missed during the 66 years are what you will find in this book.

June, 21, 2013,   *George Varuggheese, President,*
Kochi, Kerala.   *Godimages Good Governance Society*

Chapter One

The Mission Statements of the Republic of India, that is Bharat

The Preamble to the Constitution of India enshrines Mission Statements of the Indian Republic. The Preamble comprises the goals foreseen by the founding fathers of the Republic of India that could and would take India to the zenith of evolution, the human race could achieve on planet Earth. The founding fathers of the Republic of India, who, adopted and enacted the Constitution of India in the Constituent Assembly on November 26, 1949, represented the cultural and spiritual India which was known as Bharat or Bharatam since many millennia.

The committee appointed by the Constituent Assembly for drafting a new Constitution for free India, was headed by Dr B.R. Ambedkar. The committee had scrutinized more than

1

100 Constitutions of various types of governments across the world to glean the best of democratic and republican thoughts which could provide the vision, Independent India needs to follow for building up a cultural environment in which she would be able to combine the spiritual wisdom of the Vedic India and the scientific temper and innovative spirit of the modern world.

The idea of being Indians and the idea of the making of India form the key theme of the Preamble to the Constitution of India. The 395 Articles in 22 Parts and the 12 Schedules appended to them in the Constitution of India are legal frame works to give shape to the Mission Statements of the Republic of India that was committed to the people of India by the founding fathers. Whether, we, the people of India, have done justice to their trust in us, calls for a relook at the Preamble to the Indian Constitution.

The Preamble to the Constitution of India

"WE, THE PEOPLE OF INDIA, having solemnly resolved to constitute India into a SOVEREIGN SOCIALIST SECULAR DEMOCRATIC REPUBLIC and to secure to all its citizens:

JUSTICE, social, economic and political;
LIBERTY of thought, expression, belief, faith and worship;
EQUALITY of status and of opportunity;
And to promote among them all
FRATERNITY assuring the dignity of the individual and the unity and integrity of the nation;

IN OUR CONSTITUENT ASSEMBLY this twenty-sixth day of November, 1949, do HEREBY ADOPT, ENACT AND GIVE TO OURSELVES THIS CONSTITUTION."

Have we, the people of India, understood the information, our founding fathers wanted to convey to us through the Preamble to the Constitution of India, as shown above? A careful study of the current cultural environment prevailing in India would show that a majority of Indian institutions and individuals have not been able to familiarize themselves with its texts and those who have been able to familiarize themselves with them have not understood their full scope of meaning and application. Why such a situation arose will be discussed in the next chapter. Here, we will see the impact the Constitution could make on the Indian mass, by interpreting various elements of the Preamble in proper light.

We all know that Scriptures of religions play major role in the development of our faith in the religious doctrines and ritualistic disciplines that we follow to become the persons we are today. This is essentially so, because, Scriptures are basically communication media carrying purposively created messages capable of influencing the formation of a mass culture in which people are motivated to lead a life of physical, mental and spiritual uplift. Scriptures are thus communication aids for the creation of cultures that could influence successful evolution of people towards successful living.

Constitutions of countries function like Scriptures of religions. Constitutions, like Scriptures, are communication aids for the creation of cultures capable of influencing the successful evolution of people, within the scope of the

3

visions provided by their creators. While the Constitutions of countries try to create cultures favorable for certain type of governance and socio-political structures as desired by the leaders or the people, they also help create the cultural environment necessary for managing, coordinating and integrating sub-cultures of many religious, health, educational and economic institutions simultaneously.

Constitutions have a history of at least five thousand years across the world and they are more powerful aids than religious Scriptures in creating holistic and integrated cultures within the boundaries of their countries. This is because, all man-made institutions, including the religions are brought under their control for designing the development path for the populations under their charge.

Even when we think of societies and their cradle-lands, such as Aryan, Dravidian, Sumerian, Egyptian, Mayan or Greek or Roman for appreciating and admiring their civilizational heights, we have to admit that such high points in their evolution were due to the political support and direction given by the rulers in those lands to the ennobling and evolutionary intellectual and spiritual counsel provided by philosophers and prophets to their countrymen and women. Their edicts and codes of conduct for citizens inscribed on stone tablets and pillars across the length and breadth of their lands are all familiar to us.

An important aspect to note here is that these civilizations were having a common thread of belief that human beings were created in the image of God or that God had descended into the Earth realm to become men and women. While the Scriptures of Christians, Muslims and Jews proclaim that God had created men and women in His own image, the Scriptures of Indian, Chinese and other Eastern religions proclaimed that God and his created beings are one and the same. Through the ten *avatars* of Vishnu, this evolutionary process of God becoming men and men becoming gods and ascending back to God is all familiar to us.

In the history of ancient priest kings, divine kings, the medieval monarchies and the democratic governments of the people since the 18th century, the mark of success of governance was characterized by how much the principle of Universal Brotherhood of human beings and Fatherhood of God was displayed by the government of a ruler or a republic. In the case of monarchies, it is the king and his advisors who had believed in the oneness of God the Father and children of God, while in the case of democratic republics, it is the people at large who believed in the oneness existed among the people and the oneness existed between them and God. This difference in beliefs and the forms of governments are milestones humanity crossed on the road of evolution leading to successful living at total level of the society or at 100% population level.

India had Rama and Bharat as exemplary kings who had governed righteously, believing in the oneness of God and people and in the oneness among the people. But it took nearly five thousand years or more for the people at mass level to reach the higher evolved consciousness which held that all Indians are born equal and they have the inalienable right given by their Creator to evolve successfully and lead fulfilling lives. By framing the Mission Statements of their Republic in the form of the Preamble to their country's Constitution, the PEOPLE OF INDIA had not only proved their civilizational maturity but also created the best model for a republican Constitution. Indians could easily claim that in the Preamble to the Indian Constitution, they have the best model among all the Constitution models in the world though they have not made the best use of it in the application of the present Constitution of India across the length and breadth of India.

A Syntactic Analysis of the Preamble to the Constitution of India

The syntax or the order of the words of the Preamble to the Constitution of India deserves our special attention, in our efforts to fix the importance of the Constitution as a communication aid in building a proper cultural environment for inculcating the idea of being Indians and the making of India. Then only, we will be able to comprehend the semantic and linguistic implications of the messages being conveyed through the Preamble:

"We the people of India, having solemnly resolved to:

- **constitute India** into a sovereign socialist secular democratic republic;
  and to :

- **secure to all its citizens:**
  Justice, social, economic and political;
  Liberty of thought, expression, belief, faith and worship;
  Equality of status and opportunity; a*nd to :*

- **promote among them all** Fraternity assuring the dignity of the individual and the unity and integrity of the nation;

in our Constituent Assembly this twenty-sixth day of November, 1949, do hereby adopt, enact and give to ourselves this Constitution."

We the people of India, had *resolved* through an Objectives Resolution introduced by Jawaharlal Nehru in the Constituent Assembly on December 13, 1946 and passed on January 22, 1947, the territorial limits, functional nature of the Government and the objectives or goals of Independent India. Subsequent to this, the drafting committee under Dr Ambedkar had produced the draft Constitution in January 1948. After public discussion of the draft for eight months, the Constituent Assembly discussed 2473 amendments out of a total of 7635 received, on the draft Constitution between November 15, 1948 and October17, 1949. We the people of India, *adopted, enacted* and *gave to ourselves* the Constitution on November 26, 1949.

Three supreme actions are envisaged for US, THE PEOPLE OF INDIA by the resolution made by us and enshrined in the Preamble:

- To Constitute India into a SOVEREIGN SOCIALIST SECULAR DEMOCRATIC REPUBLIC; and
- To Secure to all Its Citizens, social, economic and political JUSTICE; LIBERTY of thought, expression, belief, faith and worship; EQUALITY of status and of opportunity; and

- To Promote among them all FRATERNITY assuring the dignity of the individual and the unity and integrity of the nation.

The Articles and the accompanying Schedules in the main body of the Constitution of India are the detailed legal framework to attain the goals listed in the three supreme actions. Now the question we have to ask ourselves is this: Have we attained the goals of these supreme actions? The idea of being Indians and the making of India are encrypted in these supreme actions listed above.

Obviously the answer is a big NO! Our judgment of our Republic's performance during the past sixty-three years should be based on the criteria of how far we have succeeded in fulfilling the missions listed in the Preamble to the Constitution of India. The missions contained in the Preamble target the physical, mental, spiritual and the economic well being of the people of India. Both qualitatively and quantitatively, our achievements do not exceed 30% of the targeted missions listed in the Preamble.

Major reasons for our failure in this regard, were two. One of them was our failure to build up awareness of these missions at total population level and the other reason was our failure to create social structures for implementing these missions. The failure to create the social structure will be discussed in the next chapter. Here, we are concerned with the failure to build up awareness about the urgency and importance of these missions in the minds of our people at 100% population level.

We have to believe that the founding fathers of our Republic, when encoded these missions as Preamble to the Constitution of India, were sincere in their belief that these missions which they framed were attainable and that they wanted the people of india, through generations, to strive to achieve them. We have to remember that Mahatma Gandhi, whom we revere as the Father of the Nation, had presented the social structures, for translating these missions, in the form of Hind Swaraj and Sarvodaya which the Indian political parties had dismissed as impractical.

The founding fathers, the members of the Constituent Assembly, who represented the Indian mass on the basis of religious spread, economic status and social standing, were well educated and cultured minds. By producing the set of goals for Indians, as set forth in the Preamble, they had shown that they were aware of the aspirations of Indians through the cycles of history from the ancient king Bharat to their thralldom under the British imperialism. In fact the founding fathers had captured in the Preamble, the aspirations of the soul of India, comprising all the souls of Indians, for a smooth journey towards the pinnacle of evolution, in times to come.

The time has come now for us, we the people of India, to build national consensus which will motivate the political parties to rectify their failure in building mass level awareness on the messages, the Preamble to the Constitution of India tries to convey to us. In an effort to create the proper cultural environment for the implementation of the missions of the Republic of India, as enlisted in the Preamble, we have to create the right communication model which presents the correct syntax, semantics and linguistics of the messages of the Preamble. We have seen the syntactic order of the messages in the Preamble in some of the previous paragraphs. The semantics, i.e. the meanings of the messages in the Preamble have to be understood in the correct linguistic context.

A SEMANTIC AND LINGUISTIC ANALYSIS OF THE PREAMBLE TO THE CONSTITUTION OF INDIA

'We the People of India' may look like a simple phrase beyond any problem of incomprehensibility. But, when we start pondering over its application and the consequent implications, we would know that the phrase is not all that simple but serious enough to deserve our deliberate attention. We all know that the members of the Constituent Assembly were not elected on the basis of universal suffrage but on a limited franchise. The founding fathers knew this limiting factors in the new world of democracy and republican nationalism. They consciously used this phrase not to leave any doubts in the minds of future generations of people that they were not true representatives of the people.

The Objectives Resolution moved by Jawaharlal Nehru in 1946, in the Constituent Assembly, started with these words: 'This Constituent Assembly declares its firm and solemn resolve to proclaim India as an Independent Sovereign Republic and to draw up for her future governance a Constitution; etc.' The final version of the Constitution could have started with the words, 'This Constituent Assembly having resolved . . . . gives to the people of India.'

In that case, the legitimacy of the Constituent Assembly with limited franchise would have been challenged in later years.

Many Constitution experts, in the post-Independence India, had raised this issue of lesser franchise enjoyed by the members of the Constituent Assembly and the validity of the Constitution made by them. It is this phrase, *we the people of India* which came to the rescue of the makers of the Constitution and which would prevent any future demand for a Constitution created by the members of the Indian Parliament who are elected directly by the people of Independent India.

The Constitution of India is made by the people of India for the people of India. Therefore, we must know what it is and how to use it for our benefit. We can do so, only if we empower ourselves with the knowledge that we are the owners and beneficiaries of the Republic of India whose brand value is as great or small as we think of ourselves collectively and what we make of ourselves collectively because, we are the India. Yes, India is basically, the cultural, spiritual and socio-economic India occupied by the Indians rather than the geographic India. Our cultural, spiritual and socio-economic identities are our real identities as Indians, rather than the identity of our being citizens of the geographic India.

How successfully are we managing these combined Indias? To manage the combined cultural, spiritual and socio-economic Indias, how successfully are we managing our representatives in the Legislature, Executive wing of the Government, Judiciary and the Police? Ultimately, the idea of being Indians and the making of India are located in the management of our representatives in these wings of the Government and the management of the institutions they are responsible for managing.

Another aspect related to the meaning of *we the people of India* is the balancing of the different senses in its different linguistic versions! When we use the word *Bharat* as in all Indian vernacular languages, in place of India, the semantic picture changes. Bharat is a land occupied by people who are at a higher level of health, prosperity and peace nurtured by the cultural, socio-economic and spiritual environment created by sages, saints, seers and their ardent followers from the ruling class, from ancient times! By using the word, *Bharat* in the Indian language versions of the Constitution, and also alongside the word, 'India' in Article 1, of the English version, the founding fathers of the Republic of India had made their intention of keeping the semantic picture of Bharat to be consistently integrated with that of India.

The phrase, *we the people of India* in the Preamble conveys the idea that the people of the Republic of India had a great historic background inherited from Vedas, Rishis and great rulers such as Bharat. Likewise, it conveys the idea that they have to build their future with the three supreme actions suggested further in the Preamble.

Finally, the most important idea, the phrase, *we the people of India* conveys is the sense of oneness of the people of India. Though Indians had inherited the wisdom of the Vedic literature which proclaimed that they and their Creator are not two entities but one and insisted on the common oneness existed among the people, as a society, they have been practicing caste system and discriminatory social customs towards lower castes for centuries. The founding fathers knew this and in the Independent India they shaped, they wanted the Vedic concept of oneness of humanity to prevail. The Preamble is the proof of it. But unfortunately, people are not mentally integrated with all social groups and caste conscious behavior is rampant. In the Economic Survey of 2012, presented in the Indian Parliament by Mr. Pranab Mukherjee, when he was the Indian Finance Minister, said that the root cause of India's socio-economic problem can be attributed to the lack of the sense of oneness among Indians that could have reduced the level of corruption that ravaged India at present.

The word, **Sovereign** found a place in the Preamble because, the sovereignty of a nation is derived from the autonomy enjoyed by the individuals in it by virtue of their oneness with the Creator and through Him, the oneness and brotherhood of all mankind. Indian Republic's motto, *'satyameva jayate'* quoted from Mundaka Upanishad, proclaims the triumph of this truth: Every individual's evolution is the sovereign domain of the Creator and His law of evolution. It is the duty of the State to aid the individuals to manage their sovereign evolution. The truth dealt with in Mundaka Upanishad is *brahman* which simultaneously is the Creator, the source of creation, the created worlds and beings, the process of evolution and their culmination through cycles of evolution. Emperor Ashoka whose Lion Capital was used along with 'satyameva jayate' as India's emblem, had given up the conquests of worlds and surrendered himself to the duty of aiding the evolution of not only his subjects but the whole of humanity after knowing the truth, the *brahman* through the teachings of Buddha.

The word **Socialist** was not in the original texts of 1949 but was added by 42nd Amendment of the Constitution of 1976. Nehru's plan of an economy on a socialistic pattern of society, was passed in the Avadi meeting of the Congress Party on August 14/15, 1955. The idea to "wipe every tear from every eye", was the main message of the Avadi Congress.

"I must frankly confess that I am a socialist and a republican and am no believer in kings or princes or in the order which produces the modern kings of industry, who have greater power over the lives and fortunes of man than even the kings of old, and whose methods are as predatory as those of the old feudal aristocracy. I recognize, however, that it may not be possible for a body, constituted as is the National Congress, to adopt a full socialistic program. But we must realize that the philosophy of socialism has gradually permeated the entire structure of society the world over and almost the only points in dispute are the pace and the methods of advance to its full realization. India will have to go that way too, if she seeks to end her poverty and inequality, though she may evolve her own methods and may adapt the ideal to the genius of her race," Nehru had stated at AICC session at Lahore, in 1929.

Our Father of the Nation, Mahatma Gandhi also advocated his version of socialism based on the *Ramarajya* model which he presented as *sarvodaya* and *swaraj*. Gandhian socialism advocated parity in wages of people engaged in physical labor and intellectual careers as the needs of their families were same. Gandhi was opposed to State monopoly of economy. The most attractive feature of his socialistic doctrine was his vehement advocacy of village republics, or Panchayats with autonomy enough to create prosperity and peace for people of all communities on equitable basis.

With a liberalized economy tuned to the global market economy, for India, what would be the meaning of socialism? Is it related only to the ownership of production and distribution by the State or is it related to the equitable distribution of wealth or is it a social commitment shared by the people for the welfare of every member of the society at total level? The spirit of oneness is what the Constitution is asking from us!

In January, 2008, a public interest litigation (PIL),filed by a Kolkota based NGO, seeking Supreme Court's intervention in deleting the word 'socialist' from the Preamble was dismissed by a 3-member bench headed by the then Chief Justice, K.G. Balakrishnan defining the meaning of socialism as that of the welfare of the society. Socialism is already built in the objective clauses of the Preamble: 'to secure to all its citizens: Justice, social, economic and political, Equality of status and of opportunity; and to promote among them all Fraternity assuring the dignity of the individual and the unity and the integrity of the nation . . .' What we have to decide as a modern society is whether we have to aim and work for the welfare of the total society or only the educated middle and upper classes as is happening now?

All the development planning and implementation during the past six decades in India helped mainly the middle and upper classes in the Indian society as the benefits of development trickling down to the lower classes were blocked by mental barriers imposed by traditional caste restrictions. The proof is in the demand of affected sections for reservation of fixed quota in Government jobs and educational seats over the years.

The word **Secular** is a much misunderstood word. Its Latin root *saeculum* pertains to generations or age-long event and matters related to the evolution of the material world rather than the spiritual invisible world. The word religion also has its root in Latin and it means 'to bind' and therefore in English it pertains to doctrines which bind people together in groups on matters of spiritual evolution. The word, *secular* does not mean irreligious or non-spiritual. But, being secular means, caring and loving the larger social or national entity which is formed with many sub-groups of religions and castes. A religious person who does not love the whole society is not spiritual. A secular person who loves the whole society is spiritual and he or she need not be adherent of a particular religion. Similarly, a member of a particular religion is secular, if he or she loves the larger society of many religions.

Indian society consists of many religious groups but, it marches forward as one society through generations and still it retains its identity as India. Otherwise, we cannot imagine that our founding fathers wanted the people of India, Bharat, the land of Veda and Rishis to be irreligious and unspiritual in our dealings with ourselves and our fellowmen and women!

The spirit of secularism is the spirit of universal brotherhood conveyed by the doctrine of *advaita* taught by the Upanishads which was reemphasized by Sri Sankaracharya in the 8th century AD. *Advaita* concept which states that the Creator has become the created forms and consciousness, has two aspects of evolutionary process involved in it. One relates to the spiritual or consciousness aspect while the other relates to the material aspects affecting the whole society generations after generations. Secularism is related to the material evolution of the human society as a whole. Both these aspects of *advaita* are running through all the missions enshrined in the Preamble to the Constitution of India.

Indian society was secular from time immemorial. Christianity and Islam were received with open arms by the Indians almost simultaneously as they were being established in their own lands of origin. Christians and Muslims in Kerala are as old as their religions. In India, there are many festivals or pilgrimages jointly conducted by Hindus, Muslims and Christians. This is as it should be but, this secularism was existent centuries before our Constitution came into being!

Similarly, the word, ***Democratic*** is also not understood properly by the majority of people of India. Text book definitions of the word 'democracy' and the many interpretations of democracy attributed to many ancient and recent social and political philosophers have not completed the full spectrum of possible meanings and relevance of 'democracy'! Every available definition is related to the governance of political or social groups and organizations. No one had thought that ***democracy*** also could relate to self governance by individuals. In fact major parts of intellectual enquiry and expenditure of time by people should be focused on self-governance by individuals for having a grip on the correct meaning of ***democracy*** and its impact on the evolution of the human race. Group governance such as a municipality, panchayat, state or federation of states or even business and other social organizations, cannot succeed without conscious management of self-governance by individuals in these groups.

Self governance is the management of one's own evolution in tune with the self-governing, goal-directed evolution of the Universe. Religion is the predominant institution which was created by evolved minds to help individuals in managing their self-governance. Governments, whether by priest kings, divine kings, enlightened monarchies or various types of democratic or non-democratic republics were and are conscious, deliberate creations by evolved minds of their times to support the self-governance efforts of people by providing them with sustenance for health care, education, housing, commerce, income generation, infrastructure, ecological management, relief and rehabilitation and social harmony.

The best understanding of how *democracy* is concerned with self-governance of individuals can be had from Thomas Jefferson's famous draft of the Declaration of American Independence:

"We hold these truths to be self evident, that all men are created equal, that they are endowed by their Creator with certain unalienable rights, that among these are Life, Liberty, and the Pursuit of Happiness—That to secure these rights Governments are instituted among men, deriving their power from the consent of the governed, . . ."

Thomas Jefferson's proclamation of self evident truths reflects the proclamation of eternal verities held out by Upanishads and the Old Testament Bible, through their doctrine of *advaita*. Old Testament Bible, which is common to Jews,

Christians and Muslims had proclaimed that God had created men and women in His own image while Upanishads whose teachings are akin to all Eastern religions had proclaimed that the Creator and the created are one, not two! Every human individual indeed is a god in evolution according to both Bible and Upanishads.

The word, **democracy** has originated from Greek root *demokratia*, a combination of *demos* (people) and k*ratos*(rule) and obviously, we cannot imagine a smooth rule by people if the individual is not properly self-governed! It is from the oneness of men and women with the Creator that they have derived a state of equality among themselves and the power for each one to rise to his or her divine height in health, prosperity and peace!

A Republic is the best form of government to ensure the rise of each individual, man or woman, rich or poor or young or old to his or her divine heights of health, prosperity and peace. The word, **republic** has its root in Latin phrase res publica which means public affair. In concept, thus, a republic is a state that is run by people's consent. If democracy is the rule by the self-governed public, republic is the structural form of the democratic rule. In Plato's *Republic,* the earliest work on the philosophical discussion on the concept of republican governance for managing man's earthly and spiritual development, this enquiry of what could be the best republican structure is visible.

Plato, a mystic philosopher trained in the Pythagorean mysticism and metaphysical practices, was trying to structuralize the *advaita* doctrine, through his work, *Republic,* so that people at total societal level or national level will get an aid to maximize their evolution, both physical and spiritual, through such a structure—a *republic!* The mystical brotherhood *semicircle* established by Pythagoras and the *academy* established by Plato were more or less models of *republics* in small size. The core teachings and practices of these *mini-republics* were very close to the teachings and practices of monastic orders of ancient India. Bertrand Russell, in his book, *The History of Western Philosophy,* had alluded to Pythagoras having visited India and modeling some of his teachings on the basis of Indian spiritual traditions. Bertrand Russell also had mentioned that Plato had also introduced in his *academy,* many of India's core spiritual teachings, including doctrine of reincarnation, which were essentially techniques to conduct one's life on correct evolutionary path.

We must remember that majority of the founding fathers of United States of America were members of either Masonic or Rosicrucian Fraternities, mystical societies similar to the ones Pythagoras and Plato had followed. The Declaration of Independence and the Constitution of America written by them are best models for managing the material and spiritual evolution of American people at individual and collective levels.

The Constitution of India, is also a grand model for the management of the material and spiritual evolution of Indians at individual and collective levels. The progress made by the United States of America could not be achieved by India because, the Government and civil society institutions in India could not promote *democracy* and *republicanism* in a manner required by the Constitution.

For the success of any republican state, the performances of the Legislature, Executive, Judiciary and Police are important. The Executive, Judiciary and Police, Family, Education, Health, Religion, Business and Mass media institutions have to work at optimum successful level as aids or resources for the evolution of human personality at individual and total society levels. In India, the synergy generated by the interfaces of Government and social institutions are not conducive for satisfactory level of evolution of people both at individual and societal levels. We will discuss the remedy in another chapter.

The second supreme action required by us, the people of India, according to the Preamble to the Constitution, is to 'secure *JUSTICE, economic, social and political;* **LIBERTY** *of thought, expression, belief, faith and worship;* **EQUALITY** *of status and of opportunity.'* In the manner we the people of India failed to build up the cultural environment and social structures in the case of the first supreme action of constituting India into a sovereign, socialist, secular, democratic republic, we have failed to build up necessary cultural environment and social structures in respect of the second supreme action also. We will discuss, as in the case of the first supreme action, only about the cultural environment in this chapter. The failure of creating necessary social structure in case of this second supreme action will be covered in the next chapter.

The interpretation of the words, *Justice, Liberty* and *Equality* are premised on the eternal verity that the Creator and the created men and women are one and they are governed by the law of evolution to reach the divine height of health, prosperity and peace through physical, mental and spiritual development. The purposes of all formal institutions including religion and government are to serve as designs for aiding the evolution of people. Informal institutions such as the mass media also have a duty to aid the other formal institutions engaged in managing people's evolution towards happy and successful living.

The eternal verity that the Creator and the created are one or that God had created men and women in His image is at the core of all major religious philosophies embraced by mankind. Whether 'God created man in His own image' as stated in the Old Testament Bible or whether *Brahman* became *atman* as stated in Chandogya Upanishad, the creation material had to be from within God Himself or Herself as there cannot be anything outside God as that would challenge the concept of all-pervading nature of God. Therefore, God's 'creation' could only mean God's 'becoming.' The core teachings of all major religions are trying to tell the mankind that people are gods in evolution. But the people are not taking note of this all important message!

So, the why of *Justice, Liberty* and *Equality* is rooted in the eternal verity that all creations in the Universe are evolving autonomously towards their separate missions of fulfilling their individual evolutionary goals in tune with the goal-directed autonomous evolution of the Universe. Not only the humans as gods in evolution, but other lower life streams also have the same autonomy to fulfill their ultimate missions in evolution. Just like there is an inter-dependence among people as gods in evolution, there is an inter-dependence between all living and non-living units in Nature. It is these autonomy and inter-dependence between individuals in the human race and between the different living and non-living units of Nature for their individual and collective evolution, which are sought by the missions *Justice, Liberty* and *Equality* in the Preamble to the Constitution of India.

Our founding fathers have not used the words, **Life** and **Pursuit of Happiness** which the American founding fathers had used as unalienable rights endowed by the Creator, in support of their demand for a democratic republican government. The rights to *life* and *pursuit of happiness* are covered by the word **Justice** used by our founding fathers. Since democracy is premised on the self evident truth *that all men and women are created equal by their Creator,* their right to exist, evolve autonomously and attain the mission of evolution—physical, mental and spiritual perfection or health, prosperity and peace—is unalienable and sacrosanct. Unalienable and sacrosanct because, as units of the larger self-governing, goal-directed cosmic system, their evolution is also self-governing or autonomous and goal-directed for successful evolution. All human endeavors should be to aid this evolution at individual and collective levels. Then only we can do justice to ourselves and to our Creator and His or Her creation Laws.

Securing, social, economic and political *Justice,* as mandated in the Preamble to the Constitution of India, would mean securing houses, health care, education, comfortable level of income, and social harmony at 100% population level in the Republic of India. Article 21 of the Constitution of India which confers right to life should, logically enough, receive support of an array of rights without which the right to life would become meaningless. Right to property, right to health, right to food, right to education, right to income security and right to social harmony which are necessary for autonomous evolution and fulfillment in the life of every citizen, are thus subservient to the mission sought under *Justice* in the Preamble to the Constitution of India.

Those who are averse to the idea of a divine evolutionary law demanding **justice** or obedience from us in return for individual and national level happiness will be happy to know that even the singular source of origin of the Universe is central to the evolutionary theories held by scientists and other rationalists. Even if we go by the evolution theory of modern science and rational schools of thought, the human race and other life streams are subject to the demand of justice or obedience from the law of evolution operating on us. Max Planck, the father of the quantum mechanics had emphasized on the existence of a central intelligent law operating in and through the Universe. Einstein also had more or less held similar views.

The point is, people have a oneness among them through the operating law of the Universe whether we call it divine or just natural and this existential oneness among the people is the key for the successful evolution of the human race. *Justice* demanded by the law of evolution is thus, the recognition of the rights of people at total level of the society to live and evolve to their maximum potential in physical, mental and spiritual personalities.

The third supreme action commanded by the Preamble to the Constitution of India from us is *To Promote Fraternity*. (Emphasis on the words 'To Promote' is by the author) The idea conveyed by the English words is not fully reflected in their Hindi version given in the Constitution. 'To Increase Inter-relationship' is the maximum idea that we can extract from the Hindi translation of the words 'To Promote

Fraternity.' The word, Fraternity is derived from the Latin root *frater,* meaning brother. Fraternity would thus mean brotherhood and what the founding fathers wanted us to do was to promote brotherhood 'assuring the dignity of the individual and the unity and integrity of the nation.' The word 'integrity' was added in 1976 by the 42nd Amendment of the Constitution of India.

Sixty-three years away from the adoption of the Constitution of India, the Indians cannot claim any credit for having promoted **Fraternity** in their country. Else, the condition of the various segments of the Indian society would not be what it is today. Because, **Fraternity** is the key element in the smooth and successful evolution of human society both at individual and collective levels. If a central Supreme Being or an Intelligent Law operates for the successful and purposeful evolution of the Universe and its myriad of life streams and their supporting stars and planetary systems, then their inter-dependent existence can survive only if a mutual cordiality was accepted by all the actors involved. This cordiality is sensed as 'children of one Father' as far as the human beings are concerned. The purpose of evolution, the elevation of all creation back to the Creator, as existed in the Mind of the Supreme Being or at the core of the Intelligent Law, could be achieved at human level only by Universal Brotherhood and this was correctly perceived by our founding fathers.

All welfare measures advocated by religions and all egalitarian measures advocated by democratic and republican Governments across the world, have the key element of Universal Brotherhood as their cause as well as effects. Indian Constitution through its Preamble, had commanded three supreme actions from the people and all those three actions have a common goal and that is Universal Brotherhood. If a nation promotes and maintains *Fraternity,* as desired by the Preamble, then, that is the highest level of the evolution, human race could achieve on planet Earth. All physical, mental and spiritual developments and the concomitant prosperity and peace descending on humanity will be effects rather than causes of Universal Brotherhood, achieved through the promotion of *Fraternity.*

Sensing Universal Brotherhood as the end of evolution or the goal of evolutionary law on human race, evolved minds among men and women, periodically in the past, had advocated Fraternity in the day to day life of individuals and communities achieved these through the Governments of their days. They themselves lived their ideas through fraternal communities and esoteric societies and brotherhoods. In the pre-Christian world, both in the East and West, such communities existed and the Freemasons, Rosicrucians, Theosophists of the modern days are modeled on them. Likewise, in the East, especially in India and China, many esoteric groups based on the *Advaita* doctrines of the Upanishads and Taoism, are known to be active at present.

Many of the renaissance writers whose writings influenced the American and French Revolutions, were either Freemasons or Rosicrucians. A member of these organizations addresses his or her fellow member as Frator and Soror (Brother and Sister)respectively. The recent fight of Indian civil society against rampant corruption in Government and among politicians, had received moral and organizational support from fraternities owing allegiance to yoga guru Ramdev and Art of Living supremo Sri Sri Ravishankar, RSS and a host of other fraternities. Heightened consciousness of Universal Brotherhood cultivated through internet by the youth of some 26 countries of Arab-Afro-European region, had blossomed into what is known as Arab Spring, an uprising against despotic monarchies, head of governments and fanatic religious hierarchies in their countries.

The ideas of being Indians and the making of the India of our dream must put maximum premium on *Promotion of Fraternity* among the citizens of India so that well united Indians and their institutions will form a well integrated India! Whether India will be a healthy, prosperous and peaceful country will depend on what we do to *Promote Fraternity.*

SUMMING UP

The ideas of being Indians and the making of India, the India of our dream, are in entwined existence in our minds and we should have a clarity of what is what of these two abstract ideas so that we could bring them to experiential level as concrete actions. It is not the geographic India that we are longing to be proud of, though Indians sing what poet Iqbal sang that Hindustan was the best of places on planet Earth which, he himself disowned after advocating an Islamic Union which led to the creation of Pakistan. The India of our dream is an India of spectacular socio-economic-spiritual perfection, having an age-span of some five millennia or more and having among its makers, divine personalities such as Lord Rama, Lord Krishna, Lord Buddha and exemplary monarchs such as Bharat and Asoka among others supported and sustained sincerely by the citizens. The identity of such a perfect India was the creation of its rulers and the ruled in equal measure. *Vasu daiva kutumbakam* (The whole world is a family)was their motto and they prayed everyday for the whole world by chanting, *Loka samastha sukhino bhavanthu.* *Bharat matha, Dharti matha* and *Viswa matha* were symbols of the central creative mother principle adored by them. The India they lived in was their creation weaved and perfected like spiders weaving their web out of their own being.

The Constitution of India in its Preamble, enshrined the Mission Statements of the Indian Republic which actually held the ideas of being Indians and the making of India of our dream. Indians could realize the India envisioned by Gandhi and Nehru through the ideas provided in the Preamble to the Constitution of India. These ideas, crafted into the Constitution of India by the founding fathers of the Indian Republic are able to craft the build up of the healthy, prosperous and peaceful India left behind by Rama and Bharat and which, through the millennia, remained as a goal for every Indian to pursue.

The ideas of being Indians and the making of the India of our dream, bequeathed to us by our forefathers could be realized through the three Mission Statements or the three supreme goals of the Republic of India provided in the Preamble. These are:1. To constitute India into a sovereign, socialist, secular and democratic republic. 2. To secure to all its citizens: Justice, social, economic and political; Liberty of thought, expression, belief, faith and worship; Equality of status and of opportunity; and 3. To promote Fraternity assuring the dignity of the individual and the unity and integrity of the nation. We the people of India had failed miserably to execute these Mission Statements into action.

Two reasons can be attributed to this failure: 1. We have failed to create the required social structure for carrying out the sovereign, socialist, secular, democratic and republican goals of the Preamble. 2. We have failed to create a cultural environment to motivate people to execute the Mission Statements of the Constitution contained in the Preamble.

These two reasons of our failure to execute the Mission Statements of our Republic are the subjects of discussion in the next chapter.

Both Mahatma Gandhi and Nehru believed in the possibility of having an India of socio-economic-spiritual perfection, through their own personal ideological pursuits which differed from each other's. Nehru, thought the Constitution of India which he had championed to make, would be able to make such an India while Gandhi too thought that Jawaharlal, whom he called the jewel of India, will make India a *Ramarajya* through his own socialistic pursuit. For the time being, they both were wrong. May be, we can prove them right in the long run, provided, we start now in right earnest.

Chapter Two

The Unfulfilled Mission Statements of the Republic of India

There is a song every Indian likes to hear and sing in honor and adoration of his/her mother-land and the 108-year old song still finds its pride of place in all celebrations of national importance:

> *Saare Jahan Se Acchhaa, Hindusthan Hamaara . . .*
> *(Better than the entire world, is our Hindustan,*
> *We are its nightingales, and it (is) our garden abode . . .*
> *In a world in which ancient Greece, Egypt, and Rome have all vanished without trace,*
> *Our own attributes (name and sign) live on today.)*

Poet Muhammad Iqbal of Lahore wrote this song in 1904 under the title, *Tarana-e-Hind,* when Pakistan, Bangladesh and India were in the undivided India to rouse patriotic spirit of Indians against the British. Iqbal went on a European tour in 1905 and after returning from that tour three years later as a Muslim scholar, he wrote *Tarana-e-Milli* in which he paid tribute to the Muslim unity of the world by singing, '*Chin vo Arab hamaraa hindostaaN hamaara /Muslim hain hum; watan hai saara jawhaaN hamaara . . .' (China is ours, Arabia is ours, India is ours/We are Muslims and the whole world is our homeland . . .)*

By 1930, Iqbal, already a member of Muslim League, had developed special concern for Muslim unity and he had advocated the amalgamation of Punjab, Sindh, NWFP and Baluchistan into a big North-Western province within India. Perhaps, because of this zest for a separate social identity and his association with Jinnah, he is reckoned as the brain behind the creation of Pakistan. He is called Muffakir-e-Pakistan ("The Inceptor of Pakistan") in Pakistan.

Mahatma Gandhi liked Iqbal's song so much that he used to recite it many times while he was in the Yerawada Jail in the 1930's. In 1950 the song was set to music by sitar maestro Ravi Shankar and sung by Lata Mangeshkar. The stanzas 1,3,4 and 6 out of the total 9 stanzas of the song are used as a semi-official national anthem and also as a march song of the army on national memorial days. In 1984, Indian cosmonaut Rakesh Sharma gladdened the then Prime Minister, Indira Gandhi when he described India from outer space by quoting the first line of Iqbal's song.

Iqbal who died at 61, in 1938, had abandoned his belief in nationalism when returned from his European tour in 1907, because, Islam did not approve of nationalism. His belief was that Islam was the land of God and Muslims were its dwellers under the leadership of Prophet Mohammad, forming one world-nation of Muslims.

Indians did not find the song written by the man who had conceived the idea of separate political identity for Muslims, which ultimately led to the creation of Pakistan, an anathema, nor anachronistic or antagonistic to their age-old belief in the impartial benevolence of Mother Earth to her children and sang his song all through the post-Independence era:

> "*Better than the entire world, is our Hindustan,*
> *We are its nightingales, and it (is) our garden*
> *abode . . .*"

If they sang it for rousing the patriotic fervor among the citizens of India in the pre-Independence days, it was for raising the level of the sense of self-governance among Indians and bringing back the lost glory of the India of king Bharat and emperor Asoka, that they have been singing it in the post-Independence days.

How far have we, Indians been able to make India a better place than other lands on planet Earth? Here is the answer: The latest Human Development Report for 2013 released by UNDP has ranked India at 136 among 187 nations. The ranking system known as Human Development Index constructed with factors of progress made by member nations of UN in areas of health, education and standard of living on yearly basis, was introduced in 1990 by UNDP and is recognized by members of UN as a handy measurement tool for assessing the effectiveness of governance measures implemented by governments across the world.

HDI was the brain child of Dr Mahabub Ul Haq, a Pakistani who in association with Dr Amartya Sen of India had perfected it for use by UNDP. HDI is considered to be a better yardstick than the traditional GDP for measuring the qualitative progress made by nations across the world. Factors considered by UNDP for gauging the socio-economic progress such as the per capita income, assets and property owned by individuals, life expectancy at birth and nutritional intake of citizens, quality of education and the number of years spent in schools, are better indicators of human development in a country than the economic figures of GDP.

India with the ranking of 136, is behind Sri Lanka's 97 and China's 101 rankings. Bhutan stood at 141 and is ahead of Pakistan and Bangladesh who stood at 146 in the HDI list of 2013. A point to remember is that India slipped two points in 2013 from that of 2011 which was at 134. What is the significance of this low ranking of India on the HDI? It is simply this: We have to go a long way before we could claim that we are the best. If we want to fool ourselves, we can still sing *'saare jehaan se acchha, hindustan hamaraa'* when 80% of our people live a life of deprivation in varying degrees. Either, they have no houses or land of their own or those who have, live in houses which are only qualified to be called slums. They are under-nourished and anaemic and sickness-prone. Half of their children do not see five summers, having born under-weight, to malnourished mothers. They themselves are under-educated or illiterate and their children also are poorly educated or child-laborers. Their monthly income varies from a paltry Rs.900 to Rs.7500 with a median family income of Rs.3500 per month.

You may wonder, why I display these figures? Well, you and I are the lucky ones to belong to the 20% of India's population which is articulate enough to control the economic activities to its favor. Nobel Laureate economist, Prof. Amartya Sen, in an interview to Times of India's Asha Rai, recently said that 20% of the Indian population who is articulate and influential enough, manages to get their needs catered to by the Government. People in this section are doing pretty well and are perfectly happy according to him. He said he did not think that there was enough clarity on economics here in India. Obviously, he was referring to the blind allegiance to the GDP growth alone, shown by Government's economic wizards, as the panacea for people's well being and happiness. Amartya Sen who was also instrumental in devising the Human Development Index (HDI) for UNDP, said in the interview that 'human capability expansion' was also very critical to economic growth.

An appalling 80% of the Indians fell outside the benefits of the Indian economy as is being managed by our economic wizards who were trained in the classic economic theories revolving around the GDP-growth as the pivotal goal of a nation's economy. They simply believed that the gross domestic product contributed by the 20% of the people of our country, reckon the needs of the people and fulfilled them at 100% population level. They don't believe that GDP as a yardstick for social welfare is ineffective in a society where development plans have not taken the entire population as the target. They conveniently forgot the fact that the GDP-growth-advocacies were born in societies where democratic and republican or socialist consciousness were so strong that government actions for people meant population at 100% or total level. Governance structures in those societies were democratic and republican enough to translate government policies and actions at total level of the society at 100% population level.

Does this mean in India, we are not democratic and socialist conscious and our governance structures undemocratic and non-republican? 'You are crazy,' you might accuse me for making a statement like this. Well, well, holding elections at local, state and central government levels alone does not make us true democratic and republican society. If we were truly democratic and republican, we would not have had the situation of 20% prosperity and 80% poverty in our society.

Are our political parties truly democratic and republican? Are our bureaucracy democratic and republican? Are our judiciary democratic and republican? Are our police democratic and republican? Are we democratic and republican, with many of our social organizations structured on the basis of caste, communal and class lines?

We will get the correct answers to these questions if we answer whether these structures are designed or oriented to aid the autonomous evolution of every citizen of the Indian Republic towards happy and fulfilling lives. What Amartya Sen meant by 'human capability expansion' is the 'designing of social structures as aids for the autonomous evolution or personality development of individuals for successful living' advocated by all major religious scriptures and which became core objectives of democratic and republican political theories.

The etymology of the word, 'economy' which had its origin in the Greek root word, '*oikomenein*' meaning, 'to manage Earth as a household or a habitat' proves Amartya Sen's point of view that 'human capability expansion' is crucial to the understanding of economy and economics. Incidentally, the words 'ecumenism' and 'ecology' also have their roots in the Greek word, '*oikomenein.*' These etymological premises make it amply clear that economy is the management of human habitation on planet Earth, through the journey of evolution using our skills in ecumenism and ecological prudence. All human endeavors necessary for aiding the evolution of people at the level of total human society is implied by this definition of economy. Those who manage the nations, states, local communities and family house-holds, will have to keep the unity or oneness of mankind existing in the oneness of the law of evolution in view, while managing the affairs of people under them. The secret of success in life whether at individual or group level, is to be sought in managing the unity of mankind in the diverse economic activities we undertake at individual and group level.

When we manage the economy of our beloved nation, India, that is Bharat, what we are doing is the management of the evolution of our people at total population level from north to south and from east to west by managing their needs of housing, food, clothes, health care, education, steady income, entertainment, social harmony and cultural and spiritual growth. Now, production, distribution and consumption of goods and services necessary for meeting these needs of our people have to be equitable at 100% population level, if we claim our society is a sovereign, socialist, democratic and republican one. Our measuring tool should be able to find out whether all our people have been able to meet these needs in optimum quantity and quality. GDP is not a suitable measurement since India's growth is restricted to its middle and upper classes who form the 20% of the population, as Amartya Sen had indicated. But, why only 20% of our population had benefited from the economic activities we have been following since 1950? Let us find out.

We Failed to Constitute India into a Sovereign, Socialist, Secular, Democratic Republic!

Have I made an outlandish statement? No, friends, I have made only a statement of reality prevailing in our country today. On the occasion of India completing 50 years since its Independence, Penguin India commissioned a book on India's performance as an Independent nation. The author, Pavan K Varma, a practicing diplomat attached to India's Ministry of Foreign Affairs, had brought out the shocking and shameful reality that the fruits of India's governance since Independence, were cornered by its middle class. The book titled, *The Great Indian Middle Class,* accused the Indian middle class constituting about 15 to 20% of the population, of shamelessly subverting India's goal of an egalitarian society by using the nation's democratic governance machineries and electoral processes for its selfish interests. Economic liberalization has only created more opportunities for the middle class to pursue its self interests and distance itself brutishly from the lesser fortunate 80% of the population.

Sixteen years later, in 2013, the situation has only worsened. The UNDP's Human Development Report for 2013 and

Amartya Sen's reproof of current economic situation in India are the proofs of this worsened situation.

You will recall the discourse we have had in the first chapter, about the three supreme actions the founding fathers of our august republic had listed as the Mission Statements of the Indian Republic, as contained in the Preamble to the Constitution of India. The idea of being healthy, prosperous and peaceful Indians and the making of India into a habitat of healthy, prosperous and peaceful Indians are encrypted into these Mission Statements. As Amartya Sen and Pavan K Varma had pointed out, these missions worked for only 20% of the people of India as if the founding fathers of our republic who made the Constitution of India had made it for the middle class!

If we say that the members of the Constituent Assembly who debated and drafted the Constitution of India were mostly from the middle and upper classes and they handed over the Constitution for implementation to those who belonged to the middle and upper classes, will it reveal anything as to why only 20% of the people, the middle class, benefited from the total governance activities in our country? Yes, if their middle class mentality and attitudes prevented them from translating the egalitarian, democratic and republican missions of the Republic of India enshrined in the Constitution of India!

Is the mentality of the middle class in India so self-seeking and self-serving that it is insensitive to the survival throes of the under-privileged fellow Indians forming 80% of the population? Pavan K Varma in his book had asserted so and he had warned it to be wary of the writing on the wall of serious repercussions that might be unleashed by the suffering

80%! In 1997, when he wrote the book, *The Great Indian Middle Class,* perhaps, he had the premonition of a clamor for a second revolution, of which Anna Hazare and Swami Ramdev talked and campaigned for some 14 years later.

How callous and cruel the Indian middle class could become in its pursuit of self aggrandizement has been brought out in bold relief by film star Aamir Khan through his weekly reality TV show, *Satyameva Jayate* which went on air in May, 2012. All key institutions of the Indian society are decadent and corrupted to the core with the corroding influence of the middle class' pursuit of self aggrandizement. Aamir Khan, seemingly worried at the appalling moral decadence of the Indian society across the length and breadth of the country, painstakingly probes the crucial issues with the intention of finding solutions which Independent India failed to tackle so far.

Aamir's partner in the reformative television crusade, *Satyameva Jayate* was Reliance Foundation which according to its chair-person, Nita Ambani, is on a mission of making a new India by removing poverty, illiteracy, ill-health and overall cultural lethargy. Now the question is whether the missionary spirit shared by both Aamir Khan and Nita Ambani will find fruition in a reasonable time frame? Because, the collective soul of India had started wilting in the polluted air of corruption, not yesterday or yester-year but a few hundred years ago when foreign countries started coming one after another to conquer and loot its assets.

A society that passively adjusts itself by own consent or by coercion to the vileness and craftiness of the governments of the conquering countries, will by necessity have to sell its soul for buying peace. Whether, under Mughal, French, Portuguese, Dutch or British rule, this was what the controlling sections i.e. the upper and middle classes of our society did. After the marauders left our shores, our people who control the Republic of India still continue to display the traits of their departed masters! Our collective soul requires total repair.

TV programs like *Satyhameva Jayate* by Aamir or mass campaigns such as the one for Lok Pal by Anna Hazare or Black-money repatriation demanded by Swami Ramdev will have only limited impact as far as making a new India as envisioned in the Preamble to the Constitution of India was concerned.

A total repair of the collective soul of India would have resulted from the implementation of the first supreme action envisioned in the Preamble to the Constitution of India i.e. 'constituting India into a sovereign, socialist, secular, democratic republic.' The founding fathers had two opportunities to carry out this prime mission: one, creating the Articles of the Constitution, keeping the objectives covered under it in view and two, creation of appropriate social structures for constituting India into a sovereign, socialist, secular, democratic republic. If we examine the first one, i.e. the 395 Articles purported to have been created to translate the missions of the Preamble into actions, we find, they fail to meet that objective.

The right to life ensured in Article 21 is meaningless unless, a host of other rights are ensured to citizens such as the right to food, shelter, education, health care, secured income and social harmony. Moreover, state claiming right to kill by making law for it, is denial of sovereignty of individuals who create the state as design for their own evolution towards successful living. Since, democracy is premised on the self evident truth that all men and women are created equal and they have the inalienable right given by their Creator, to live and evolve in tune with the evolution of the Cosmos, any law made to deprive a person of his or her life, thus denying him or her rightful evolution, cannot be viewed as democratic. Only corrective and reformative punishments and not capital punishments are justified in accordance with the missions stated in the Preamble to the Constitution of India.

There were wide-spread criticisms from the very beginning that the Constitution of India was written by lawyers for lawyers! An impartial reading will not escape that criticism echoing in our minds. Articles have been constructed in such a way that those who do not want democracy or those who would like to support feudal, fascist bourgeoisie causes, could twist them in their favor. India's post-Republican career amply demonstrates that across all the institutions of our society, more of feudal-fascist bourgeoisie practices are rampant rather than the sovereignty of people, socialism, secularism and democracy. The more than three crores of cases pending in the Indian courts as of 2012 for time-frames ranging from one to thirty years or more with a good percentage of this figure languishing in jails for more than five years awaiting the commencement of trials or even awaiting hearing what their crimes were, or even bails being denied merely due to the whims and fancies of officers trained under the aegis of the feudal-fascist bureaucracy bequeathed by the imperialist government of Britain, is a phenomenon born out of the mismatch between the democratic aims of the Indian Republic recorded as the Preamble and the limited variable results obtainable from the many Articles of the Indian Constitution.

When we look through the twenty-two parts of the Constitution of India, what we find is that the logic behind the linkages of the twenty-two parts in to a whole, clearly demonstrates a tendency to appreciate the merit and sufficiency of whatever institutions created by the imperial government of Britain and continue with them, rather than putting in efforts to create new republican structures capable of translating the Mission Statements of the Indian Republic contained in the Preamble. We get the impression that the founding fathers wanted only the British to go from India and not their feudal, fascist governance structures and methods.

But what should surprise us is the fact that they thought the newly emerged independent and republican India would achieve all what they had written in the Preamble with the help of the feudal governance structures used in India by the colonial British government which, ironically, followed a parliamentary democracy at home in England!

Thus, governments at the Centre, in the states, municipalities and the panchayats and their supporting institutions such as the parliament, state assemblies, attorney general, judiciary, public service commission, election commission, comptroller and auditor general etc. provided for by the Constitution of India, lacks the republican goals of the Preamble.

Rather, the accent is on the collection of revenue which was the main function of the British government in India. Though, in March 1950, Planning Commission was created as an after-thought, its terms of reference failed to take note of the personality development as well as the socio-economic development of individuals at 100% population level, sought in the Preamble to the Constitution. The terms of reference mainly focus on the utilization of resources rather than development of people.

Britain ran the government of India to collect revenue and resources for sending them to England. Republic of India collect revenue to run the government of India. Because, the focus of the Constitution of India's lengthy body of Articles is on running a strong government for itself with the revenue collected. What is the cost of running the Government of India and the state governments? According to published data, 70% of the revenue collected by the Central and 80% of revenue collected by state governments go into running the governments at the Centre and states respectively. Out of the remaining 20 % to 30%, for every rupee spent on development activities, according to the Planning Commission itself, 83 paise goes into administration of the various schemes and projects.

According to media reports, Government officials dealing with the finances and accounts of the Government of India are seriously thinking about doing away with the dual type accounting i.e. plan and non-plan, because of the discomfiture generated by the ever rising non-plan expenditure figures! Like the British government, our government too believes that India is the government and the government is India because, the Constitution recognizes so! The Public Service Commission instituted by the Constitution of India is the proof that government workers are important because they run the Republic of India. Other work-force forming 95%

of the total workers in India working for the development of the Indian Republic are therefore ignored to the extent that a living minimum wage has not been fixed for them. Thus, when a government servant gets anywhere from Rs.15,000 per month at the minimum and 150,000 and perks at the maximum of scale, a non-government worker starts with less than Rs.1,000 and may end with anywhere between Rs. 2,000 to Rs.3,000 in his life time.

Today, a government servant can get a pension up to a lakh of rupees per month which he or she may not need for his or her daily bread, because of his or her well settled financial background solidified while in service, ably assisted by the well settled children, but which could provide for the much coveted foreign vacation, as he or she need not spend a penny on medical expenses either, as that too is paid by the government. But today, a worker in the unorganized sector of the economy, might get a special old age pension of Rs.200 to 600 per month from either the Central or state governments. He has no medical coverage for him or his family. A woman worker in the government can get 6 months' all paid maternity leave for two children and an additional paid leave for two years for helping with the examination preparation of her children when they are old enough for that. But a woman worker in the unorganized sector, will have to go through all her pregnancies with the prospect of giving birth to under-weight children who may not live to see five summers!

Under the British rule, a government worker's loyalty was precious for the treasury in England, not for the people of India. In the Republican India, the loyalty of the government worker is precious for the government, and not for the people of India as the government exists for itself on the basis of the model created by the Constitution of India—more of a revenue collection model and less of a developmental model!

The Comptroller and Auditor General of India's is a post indicating that the government is a revenue modeled government. In absence of somebody who will worry about what development was undertaken with the money collected by the government, he reigns supreme in the constellations of government functionaries whether in the bureaucracy or in the political section of the government. If he believes that the government is the Republic which the Constitution wants him to believe, he might even question the decisions of ministers elected by the people on their socialistic and democratic qualities, as to why they distribute natural resources at welfare oriented prices when they could get more revenue by auctioning them at higher prices. He is not bothered whether the mass consumption promoted by the welfare oriented fixed price will be turned into class consumption prompted by the extra profit for the government because, the Constitution promotes the government rather than the development of people.

In his support, there are sections of all political parties, the media, judiciary and civil society. Because, they jointly make the Indian middle class which chased away the British rulers and cherishingly accepted the feudal-fascist social systems left behind by them. By creating provisions for constituting a government on the British model that ruled India for three-and-half centuries under East India Company and direct monarchy in the most vicious form of fascism, the founding fathers of the Indian Constitution, have done enormous harm to their own good intentions and noble goals espoused in the Preamble. As we have seen already, they missed the opportunity of creating through the Articles of the Constitution, provisions for 'constituting India into a sovereign, socialist, secular, democratic republic.' Whatever little have been done in the area of Fundamental Rights and Parliamentary systems, were overpowered by the British revenue model of governance structures provided for in other Articles.

The founding fathers have also missed the second opportunity of creating new forms of republican structures, through Act of Parliament, for 'constituting India into a sovereign, socialist, secular, democratic republic.' Independent India had paid a heavy price for this innocent oversight on the part of our founding fathers. Though Nehru had vowed many times before taking charge as the first prime minister of India, that he would have nothing to do with the ICS model of administrators in Independent India, he hardly could do anything to change the style of IAS which followed the practice of ICS without much visible change in structure and functions. Similarly, by allowing the Judiciary and Police structure and practices as existed in the British rule to continue as they were without any change, have nullified the grand objectives listed in the Preamble. It is obvious that the Majority in the Constituent Assembly did not allow Nehru to have his way.

K.M. Munshi, a member of the Constituent Assembly had been quoted in Pavan K Varma's book as saying that most of his colleagues had looked up to the British model as the best choice for Independent India's governance as it had been built over a period of more than a century. Why should we go for a new experience, he and his colleagues felt? Even Dr. S. Radhakrishnan had admired the administrative and law and order systems established by the British colonial government over the years in India, on the eve of India's assumption as a Republic. When Dr. Man Mohan Singh, India's current Prime Minister repeated the eloquent praise of the British systems of administration and judiciary functioning in India, at Oxford on July 8, 2005 while receiving an honorary degree from his alma mater, it was an eloquent confirmation of his country's middle class being in total agreement with the founding fathers in continuing with the British governance systems in running the republican India.

Opposition parties in India had ridiculed Dr Singh for his lavish praise of the British model of government, even though they had made no sincere effort to challenge him with a better alternative republican model of governance. All political parties, especially the Bharatiya Janata Party had time and again accused the Congress Party of ruling India for the middle class all these years. But, no party had pin-pointed or attributed the country's low human development index to the British model of governance, adopted by our founding fathers.

In modern vocabulary, a scam stands for a fraudulent act or set of acts involving personal gains of the perpetrators of such acts. When a group of leaders after openly declaring democratic and republican goals for their country in the Preamble to the Constitution of their country, make detailed provisions for continuing with the feudal, oppressive governance systems of their erstwhile colonial masters, that can be called a socio-economic-spiritual scam sculpted on behalf of the Indian middle class against the 80% of the population which was excluded from the development agenda of the country. These leaders were, and their followers are, the products of a smart scam contrived by Lord Macaulay and his bosses in London against the Indian masses when they chalked out and implemented the education policy for the Indian sub-continent way back in 1835 and the Indian Criminal Procedure and Penal Code in 1858-1860. Though, Lord Macaulay drafted the Indian Criminal Procedure and Penal Code before he left for England in 1838, they were implemented only in 1858 after the historic uprising by soldiers of East India Company's army unit in Meerut.

The education policy introduced by Lord Macaulay in 1835 was so effective in winning over the Indian middle class to the side of Britain not only during its rule in India, but also throughout the post-Independence India, till today. In his minute on the introduction of English as the medium of higher education with contents from European culture and literature, which, Lord William Bentinck, Governor General of India readily accepted, he wrote: "We must at present do our best to form a class who may be interpreters between us and the millions whom we govern,—a class of persons Indian in blood and color, but English in tastes, in opinions, in morals and in intellect. To that class we may leave it to refine the vernacular dialects of the country, to enrich those dialects with terms of science borrowed from the Western nomenclature, and to render them by degrees fit vehicles for conveying knowledge to the great mass of the population." In support of his argument, he further wrote:

"I have no knowledge of either Sanskrit or Arabic. But I have done what I could to form a correct estimate of their value. I have read translations of the most celebrated Arabic and Sanskrit works. I have conversed both here and at home with men distinguished by their proficiency in the Eastern tongues. I am quite ready to take the Oriental learning at the valuation of the Orientalists themselves. I have never found one among them who could deny that a single shelf of a good European library was worth the whole native literature of India and Arabia. The intrinsic superiority of the Western literature is, indeed, fully admitted by those members of the Committee who support the Oriental plan of education."

114 years later, by 1949, the middle class was so molded and manipulated by the European culture administered dose by dose through the education system introduced by Lord Macaulay, that its representatives, the founding fathers of the Indian Republic, not only forgot and forgave the more than 300 years of exploitation of the Indians by the British, but willingly yoked the Republic of India to the feudal colonial governance systems used by the British.

As a proud custodian of this tradition, Dr. Man Mohan Singh, India's Prime Minister echoed the warm sentiments of the Indian middle class towards Britain for running a colonial government in India so efficiently and effectively: At the acceptance speech delivered by him after receiving a honorary degree on July 8, 2005, he said: "There is no doubt that our grievances against the British Empire had a sound basis for, as the painstaking statistical work of the Cambridge historian Angus Madison has shown, India's share of world income collapsed from 22.6% in 1700, almost equal to Europe's share of 23.3% at that time, to as low as 3.8% in 1952. Indeed, at the beginning of the 20th Century, "the brightest jewel in the British Crown" was the poorest country in the world in terms of per capita income. *However, what is significant about the Indo-British relationship is the fact that despite the economic impact of colonial rule, the relationship between individual*

*Indians and Britons, even at the time of our Independence, was
relaxed and, I may even say, benign."(Emphasis: mine)*

Obviously, the Macaulay effect on the Indian middle class
who had occasion for social intercourse with Britons in India
and England both inside and outside the government circles
is implied in the speech. Read further:

"This was best exemplified by the exchange that Mahatma
Gandhi had here at Oxford in 1931 when he met members
of the Raleigh Club and the Indian Majilis. The Mahatma
was in England then for the Round Table Conference and
during its recess, he spent two weekends at the home of A.D.
Lindsay, the Master of Balliol. At this meeting, the Mahatma
was asked: "How far would you cut India off from the
Empire?" His reply was precise—"From the Empire, entirely;
from the British nation not at all, if I want India to gain and
not to grieve." He added, "The British Empire is an Empire
only because of India. The Emperorship must go and I should
love to be an equal partner with Britain, sharing her joys and
sorrows. But it must be a partnership on equal terms." This
remarkable statement by the Mahatma has defined the basis
of our relationship with Britain. What impelled the Mahatma
to take such a positive view of Britain and the British people
even as he challenged the Empire and colonial rule? It was,
undoubtedly, his recognition of the elements of *fair play
that characterized so much of the ways of the British in India.*
Consider the fact that an important slogan of India's struggle
for freedom was that "Self Government is more precious
than Good Government". That, of course, is the essence of
democracy. *But the slogan suggests that even at the height of our
campaign for freedom from colonial rule, we did not entirely*

reject the British claim to good governance. We merely asserted our natural right to self-governance.

Today, with the balance and perspective offered by the passage of time and the benefit of hindsight, it is possible for an Indian Prime Minister to assert that India's experience with Britain had its beneficial consequences too. Our notions of the rule of law, of a Constitutional government, of a free press, of a professional civil service, of modern universities and research laboratories have all been fashioned in the crucible where an age old civilization met the dominant Empire of the day. These are all elements which we still value and cherish. Our judiciary, our legal system, our bureaucracy and our police are all great institutions, derived from British-Indian administration and they have served the country well.

Of all the legacies of the Raj, none is more important than the English language . . . . Today, English in India is seen as just another Indian language . . . *Our Constitution remains a testimony to the enduring interplay between what is essentially Indian and what is very British in our intellectual heritage."(Italics mine).*

I have extensively used the speech of Dr. Man Mohan Singh, only to show the Macaulay effect on the Indian middle class. Under the well planned scheme of Britain through Lord Macaulay, India lost its identity to the extent that, it started savoring its servility even after Independence through the continuation of British systems of feudal governance for managing its own democratic and republican goals. If Dr. Man Mohan Singh sounded happy in praising Britons for what they have done to colonial India, it was the expression of the gratified Indian middle class, the 20% that runs India for its own glory.

We must not forget the fact that Britain, a nation owing allegiance to Christ, who taught on universal brotherhood and good neighborly living like the good Samaritan, went about enslaving one fourth of world's nations for embellishing itself with rich life styles and standard. A nation boasting of parliamentary democracy with hereditary monarchy, House of Commons and House of Lords representing the common people and the aristocracy, Britain had no compunction to allow millions to die of famine not once but many times during its colonial rule in India, through greedy over-taxation and callous withholding of relief measures during drought seasons. Many Western authors had written about Britain's brutal behavior during its Indian rule, but our intelligentsia did not care to take note of it because of the Macaulay effect.

In his speech in the House of Commons on July 10, 1833, canvassing extension for East India Company's rule in India and introduction of English and European culture for civilizing the 'pagans' and 'heathens' of India who were compared to the Europeans before 5th century, Macaulay also was critical of British officials in India who were not supporting Christian missionaries in their works in India. Though he was in approval of British government's impartial role in the spread of Christian religion in India, his allusion of Indians being in the state of Europeans prior to the 5th century, it was clear that he wanted Indians to be like Europeans of post-5th century when Christian 'civilization' was introduced throughout Europe by Roman emperor Theodosius.

Macaulay succeeded in civilizing Indians with European culture to the extent that India's founding fathers and now Dr. Man Mohan Singh could perceive that Britain had been providing good governance to India, though not self governance which she demanded. Before East India Company came to India in 1608, England had flourished on thriving international slave trade for many centuries. During East India Company's rule from 1757 till 1857 and British government's direct rule from 1858 to 1947, Indians were treated as slaves in respect of wages of workers, long working hours, lack of provision for adequate food and medicine supplies. During this phase, as Dr. Man Mohan Singh quoted from Cambridge historian Angus Madison's economic figures, India's share of world income decelerated from 23% to 3% even though, England was the epicenter of the Industrial Revolution which occurred during the 1750-1850 period. Because, India was used as a mine of raw materials and a market of finished British goods.

The verdict is clear to all of us: British India continues in all its glory with the same fair play, rule of law, education system and schools, judiciary and civil service administration. The first supreme action contemplated by the Preamble to the Constitution of India i.e. 'to constitute India into a sovereign, socialist, secular, democratic republic' is yet a goal to be achieved.

We Failed to Secure to All Our Citizens, JUSTICE, social, economic and political ; LIBERTY of thought, expression, belief, faith and worship and EQUALITY of status and of opportunity.

On February 22, 2012, in Nashik, addressing the students of a school run by the Rashtriya Swayamsevak Sangh (RSS), its supreme chief, Mohan Bhagwat said:

"After Independence, the dominance of rich and powerful people in politics and rising inflation have worsened the country's situation, which is worse than what it was during the British rule . . . All political parties were in power some time or the other during the last 64 years since Independence, but the situation has not improved. Hence, citizens must introspect over what went wrong."

Mr Mohan Bhagwat heads an organization having 6 million members engaged in discovering India for Indians as they felt, because of the long British presence in India, especially due to the Macaulay effect, Indians have lost their self respect and identity. Moreover, by running an organization which has also Vedic dictum, "*vasudhaiva kutumbakam*" as its guiding principle, Mohan Bhagwat's thought processes deserve our attention. It is this one concept, i.e. that the 'whole world is a big family,' the equivalent of *vasudhaiva kutumbakam*, which is upheld by the demand of the Preamble to the Constitution of India, 'to constitute India into a sovereign, socialist, secular, democratic republic.' Because, a 'world family' concept inheres practices of sovereignty, socialism, secularism, democracy and republican ecumenism, the essential qualities in which the autonomous evolution of individuals takes place. Conversely, we cannot run a democratic republic without imbibing the ideals of *vasudhaiva kutumbakam,* as the sole objective of a republican government is to manage the autonomous evolution of every citizen of the republic.

Mr Bhagwat has asked us to introspect over what went wrong during the past 65 years since Indian Independence and we have already seen what went wrong: As Dr. Man Mohan Singh had stated at Oxford University in 2005, the Indian middle class which steered the freedom struggle wanted only to take out power from the Britons into its own hands and as regards their rule in India, the Indian middle class had already given certificate of good governance to the Britons. It is this perception on the part of our founding fathers in the Constituent Assembly, which had prompted them to create provisions in the Constitution for continuing the British rule in their newly emergent republic!

Mr Bhagwat has also complained that things were worse than what it was in the British India of pre-Independence because, the rich and powerful people dominated the political scene in India. Obviously, the rich and powerful have the right to join politics but what he implied was that they had cornered all the benefits of governance of the republic of India during the 65 years since Independence. Since the Constitution of India was tailor-made to continue the British made governance structures and methods in the Republic of India, it was easy for the rajas, raj-pramukhs, zamindars, land lords and feudal lords from all the 600 odd erstwhile princely states to join the ruling party, Indian National Congress and share the burden of nation building on the lines drawn by the British under whom they flourished. It was a blessing on the rebound to them actually. Nehru could not do anything, or he believed that under his leadership they were bound to obey his policies. Little did he realize that the Constitution he helped to make were administered by the British made bureaucracy which once he hated to the core of his heart, to convert his government for and by the middle class.

Mr Bhagwat also observed that all the political parties had the opportunity to be in power or share power with other allies during the past 65 years but they have done nothing to do better than what it was in the British India. Obviously, they could not do anything except perpetuating the British rule under the Indian garb given by the Constitution of India. We need not be surprised at this. If you get an opportunity, please go through the aims and objectives of our political parties. None of them have the goals listed in the Preamble as their objectives primarily or even secondarily! All of them seek to thrive on the life and times of their leaders, their missions and their visions which left the Mission Statements of the Indian Republic as contained in the Preamble to the Constitution of India, untouched.

Gandhiji knew that the Congress which was constituted to bring freedom to India needed to reorganize itself on the basis of the Mission Statements of the Indian Republic as contained in the Preamble to the Constitution of India. Historians have recorded that Gandhiji had made known this to the Congress leaders of the time but with no success. This was not surprising either, because Gandhiji's Swaraj proposal also had been rejected by Congress. But, Swaraj or Sarvodaya model of governance put forward by Gandhiji was in total compliance with the Mission Statements of the Indian Republic enshrined in the Preamble to the Constitution of India.

Somewhere, something had gone wrong with the Congress, because, the party's manifesto of 1929 drafted by Nehru which found reflection in the Mission Statements of the Indian Republic in the Preamble were not translated in the many provisions of the Constitution nor in the working program of the party in the post-Independence period:

"We believe that it is the inalienable right of the Indian people, as of any other people, to have freedom and to enjoy the fruits of their toil and have the necessities of life, so that they may have full opportunities of growth. We believe also that if any government deprives a people of these rights and oppresses them, the people have a further right to alter it or abolish it. The British government in India has not only deprived the Indian people of their freedom but has based itself on the exploitation of the masses, and has ruined India economically, politically, culturally and spiritually. We believe therefore, that India must sever the British connection and attain Purna Swaraj or complete independence . . . . We shall seek every opportunity to spread goodwill among fellowmen without distinction of caste or creed. We shall endeavor to raise from ignorance and poverty those who have been neglected and to advance in every way the interests of those who are considered to be backward and suppressed." This pledge forming part of the 1929 Congress party resolution remains unredeemed even to this very day only because, the founding fathers in the Constituent Assembly believed that they could run the Republic of India with the systems of governance used by the British colonial government. They believed those systems were good enough as they were developed by the British over a period of more than hundred years. If the British could use them to run this country successfully, then, they did not see why they could not be used by them successfully. We have already seen what K. M. Munshi, the nominated member in the Constituent Assembly had said, in an earlier section of this book. We have also read what Dr. Man Mohan Singh had said at Oxford University in 2005. Both of them were in agreement with our founding fathers.

Why did the British rule this country? Why do we rule this country? The British ruled this country to make wealth for their country. We rule this country to make the people of this country healthy, prosperous and happy at total level of the population. If these two goals were different, could the same systems of governance produce two different results? Obviously, not. Were not our leaders capable of knowing this implication? Well, this need to be explored by social scientists to determine whether there was a scam or a scandal of sociological nature!

What we can deduce from this puzzling situation is that since the governance systems being used by the Independent India belonged to the colonial India, we may get more or less the same governance which existed in the colonial British India. The implication of this deduction is that the Indian society may not have gone through much transformation from a feudal, caste-ridden, disparate, economic social order.

Obviously the life around us indicates that our society has not changed much the way we wanted in the Preamble to the Constitution of India. We wanted health, prosperity and peace at 100% population level. The second supreme action sought from us by the Preamble was **to secure Justice, Liberty and Equality for all the citizens.** On this account, we have failed terribly. What was intended to be achieved by this mission statement in the Preamble to the Constitution of India was to rebuild Indian society on equitable basis so that India would be rid of the unjust social conditions which Jawaharlal Nehru described in the manifesto he drafted for the Congress party in 1929 at Lahore.

India remaining at the bottom level of Human Development Index(HDI) i.e. at 136 out of 187, is a sufficient indication that our society has not gone through any qualitative socio-economic-cultural transformation during the period since Independence, for the majority of its people. Since HDI is composed of factors related to standard of living, education and health, we can easily judge that our society has achieved very little in these vital areas since the days of our becoming a republic.

For standard of living, factors like house, house with land, an income that can ensure purchasing power for securing foods, clothes, medicines, children's education, transportation facilities, entertainment etc are taken into account. India's middle and upper class combine which is estimated to be around 250 to 300 million of the total population of 1.2 billion, has a good standard of living, considering the factors given above.

Since houses were not covered under fundamental right, and therefore government was not obliged to provide houses to people, there was no serious data collection till recently to decide how many people have houses and how many more needed. The calculation made during the 11th Plan period i.e. 2007-2012 by the government was that India had shortage of about 27 million houses. This, at the rate of five persons per household will cover 135 million people. This figure will not hold good as the below-poverty-line(BPL) people according to the government was 37% or 400 million and BPL citizens owning houses from own sources is not imaginable at all. As the government's norms for fixing the BPL was the daily spending of less than Rs.32 by an urban citizen and Rs.26 or less by a rural citizen, 400 million is not going to be the correct figure. According to National Commission for Enterprise in Unorganized Sector, the BPL figure is 70%. According to a World Bank estimate, India needs 70 million houses. World Bank's assessment was made on the basis of the purchasing power of people who have income ranging from Rs.200,000 to 10,00000 a year. But our major enquiry is about what happened to our Mission Statements in the Preamble?

A newly independent nation makes a grand goal for itself and resolves 'to secure for all its citizens, Justice, economic, social and political.' Houses for all should have been a fundamental right of citizens. All men and women born in the land of India should have been given equal rights of having a place of their own to conduct their family lives in peace and harmony with their fellow men and women. The 900 million people falling outside the middle and upper class boundary needs intervention from the state to fulfill the Mission Statements made in the Preamble to the Constitution of India.

What is the income that can fetch a comfortable living for a citizen in India today? What is the income with which one can finance a house, send his children to school, have nutritious food and comfortable clothing for his family, spare enough for health care and some entertainment and also a little saving for taking care of emergencies? Is it Rs.32 per day and Rs.960 per month and Rs. 11520 per year? Nothing short of Rs. 15000 per month could fetch a decent life at minimum level of creature comforts at today's prices of things and services.

In this country, a decent job that ensures secured income on continuous level is not a fundamental right and therefore no governments at central or state levels are duty bound to bother about it. A house, education, health, food, clothes and entertainment are all dependent on steady and sufficient income. When the Preamble to the Constitution of India declares the mission of the republic, to secure to all its citizens, Justice—economic, social and political—then, a key set of fundamental rights have to be made absolutely inalienable from the citizens' right to live and evolve autonomously in tune with the laws of Nature. And these fundamental rights can be ensured only if a minimum living wage or income is assured to every citizen in our country.

Absence of such a right to secured income for a decent life has made half of our people under-nourished and anemic making them prone to all kind of diseases. In the Times of India of July 14, 2012, a report originated from Wardha quoted Dr Binayak Sen, the noted social equity activist as saying that according to National Nutrition Monitoring Bureau(NNMB), 37% of India's adult population is having a low body mass index (BMI) of 18.5 indicating this section of our people are famished. According to the World Health Organization, if 40% of people of a society suffers the low BMI of 18.5 or less, then that community is under chronic famine. A healthy community is that which has a BMI between 18.5 and 24.5. A BMI above 24.5 indicates obesity. Dr Binayak Sen further disclosed that among 65% of rural women, 60% of scheduled castes and tribes and 47% of children under age 5 are suffering from the low BMI of 18.5 or less. According to him, India is reeling under famine because, almost half of its citizens are in dire condition of malnutrition.

We are in a terrible situation of endangering our future generation with underdeveloped brain and its concomitant below par intellectual output which might affect India's economic and technological growth negatively. The reason is that, neural science says that if a child's brain is stunted in the first 3 years due to malnutrition, then the child's brain growth is sealed for life. India with almost half of its children under the age five, suffering from malnutrition and under-weight, there is the frightening prospect for them to have under-developed brain and consequent weak intellectual faculty.

'India's efforts to overtake China in economic development will never be possible, if half of India's future generation is exposed to the danger of undeveloped brain power caused by malnutrition among children. Because, in China, malnutrition among children under 5 years have come down heavily to 7% during the past two decades as a result of state supervision in integrated child development. India lacked such determined effort,' according to New York Times columnist David Reiff. Even in sub-Saharan Africa, the malnutrition among children up to 5 years stands at 27%, much below that of India!

Have we ever questioned ourselves, why is this happening to us in India? It is not because we do not have the money, manpower and material for managing our children's and thereby nation's health. But, it is only because of our administration inherited from the feudal British government in India. Our founding fathers and later almost all our leaders thought of Britain as a parliamentary democracy and therefore, while adopting its Indian administration machinery for running Indian parliamentary democracy, they thought they had done a smart job in saving time and money which otherwise would have cost in developing a brand new manpower set up in India.

We have not made any state level efforts in raising the standard of living in India during the last six decades and as a result half of our citizens have below average growth of body mass and half of our children under age 5 are threatened with low neural development. According to UN World Food Program, India is home to about 25 percent of the world's hungry poor. Although the country grows enough food for its people, pockets of hunger remain.

The charity organization, Bhookh Foundation from Mumbai which is associated with UN World Food Program, says that hunger is the number one cause of death in India. According to it, over 7000 Indians die of hunger every day and over 25 lakh Indians die of hunger every year.

Our warehouses are full and in fact millions of tons of food grains are rotting in the open, as Food Corporation of India's warehouses are full. Both bureaucratic and political management systems in the country are so well grooved in the British feudal governance philosophy, that to bring themselves to the egalitarian dispensation of justice and equality and fraternity is very hard indeed for our managers in the government. Therefore, grains rot, people die of hunger, anemic mothers give birth to underweight children.

"A child dies every 15 seconds in India due to neonatal diseases while 20 lakh children die before reaching their fifth birthday. Over four lakh newborns are dying every year within 24 hours of life in the country. Over 20% of the world's child deaths occur in India—the largest number anywhere in the world. One in three of all malnourished children in the world live in India. A child who has severe acute malnutrition is at least nine times more likely to die than a child who does not," according to a study report in Times of India of July 14, 2012.

In a country whose economy is mainly dependent on agriculture, one should have thought that farmers would get fair treatment from our government. But, no, thanks to our British model of governance, not only that they cannot make a decent living, but many of them are ending their lives out of helplessness. With a figure of at least 14,027 in 2011, according to the National Crime Records Bureau (NCRB), the total number of farm suicides since1995 has touched 2,70, 940. The State of Maharashtra has shown a rise in numbers yet again, logging 3,337 against 3,141 farmers' suicides the previous year (and 2,872 in 2009). Other states accounting for major farmer suicides are Madhya Pradesh, Andhra Pradesh and Karnataka.

Poor sanitation forms a major component of India's health issues.

As more than 122 million households have no toilets, and 33% lack access to latrines, over 50% of the population (638 million) defecates in the open. This is relatively higher than Bangladesh and Brazil (7%) and China (4%). Although 211 million people gained access to improved sanitation from 1990-2008, only 31% uses them. 11% of the Indian rural families dispose of stools safely whereas 80% of the population leave their stools in the open or throw them in the garbage. Open air defecation leads to the spread of diseases and malnutrition through parasitic and bacterial infections.

Public health service in India is one of the poorest among nations. India ranks among the lowest globally, with 0.9 beds per 1,000 population—far below the global average of 2.9 beds. In 2010 India had a public sector availability of one bed per 2012 persons available in 12,760 government hospitals—around 0.5 beds per 1,000 population. Sri Lanka on the other hand has 3.1 beds per 1,000 population, China 3 beds, Thailand 2.2, Brazil 2.4, USA 3.1 and UK 3.9 beds per 1,000 population. The Bhore Committee in 1948 had recommended that there should be one bed per 1,000 population. We still haven't been able to reach that target in 65 years.

India's life expectancy index also is very low. Among the 227 nations of the world, India stands at 166 with 67 years of life expectancy at birth. China stands at 99 with 75 years while Sri Lanka enjoyed 86th position with 76 years. Pakistan is slightly behind India at 171 with 66 years of life expectancy. Developed nations who occupy the first 50 positions have life expectancy rates between 80 and 90 years.

India's health problems have multiplied manifold by the pollution of river and ground water with toxic chemicals and heavy metals. The threat to the Indian society is from the indifferent and irresponsible posture of government more than from the pollution itself, because, the pollution is removable by timely action while the indifference and irresponsibility of government and political personnel are not easily removable as these traits have been inherited from the British India government tradition which was built on government centric service attitude instead of people centric service attitude.

Thousands of children with deformities are born in Punjab and Kerala where heavy use of pesticides takes place for protecting their cash and seasonal crops from pests. Almost all major rivers across the country are heavily polluted with effluents discharged by industrial plants and the ground water aquifers throughout the country thus carries toxins to agricultural fields and drinking water wells and from there to the human bodies through food and water consumed. Thousands of children die before they reach their adolescence due to malformed internal organs which were the direct results of the presence of toxins in the bodies of their parents especially, mothers.

We have just had a glimpse of the failures of the Indian society in the two vital areas i.e. standard of living and health, forming the three-pronged HDI prescribed by UNDP for measuring the progress made by nations in overall development of their people. The next in the HDI is education which is measured in a society by the literacy level it holds and the number of years a child or a person spends in the school and college. India's HDI ranking at 136 by the UNDP which considered factors of progress made in standard of living, health and education, is an indication that our society has not made much progress since its liberation from the British captivity. Not that it did not make any progress. It made progress to a level which is not much praise-worthy, considering the long period we Indians traversed since our freedom and the long journey we still have to make to reach the 100% literacy and zero percent drop-out levels.

Despite all our efforts since Independence, 25% of our population is still illiterate; only 15% of Indian students reach high school, and just 7%, of the 15% who make it to high school, complete high school years. The quality of education whether at primary or higher education is significantly poor as compared with major developing nations. As of 2012, India's post-secondary institutions offer only enough seats for 10% of India's college-age population, 25% of teaching positions at primary and secondary school and college levels nationwide are vacant, and 57% of college professors lack either a master's or PhD degree.

Right from the post-Independence period, India has been spending much below the required level on education. From 0.7% of GDP in 1950 to a little over 3% of the GDP in 2012 spent on education was not at all figures that would have ensured literacy and mental skill at 100% population level. Experts feel, at least India should be spending around 7% of the GDP or 20% of its annual expenditure on education continuously in the coming years to give quality education and mental skill at total level of the population. All developed nations spend between 5 to 10% of their GDP on education.

Thomas Babington Macaulay who was familiarly known as Lord Macaulay, introduced an education system in India in 1835 to turn out Indians who thought like Europeans while appeared like Indians. And he succeeded like hell in consuming India's self respect and self identity through the impartation of European education and cultural indoctrination through the entire spectrum of educational institutions in India, into the ashes of submissiveness and supplications to anything Western, whether, products, philosophy or pornography.

If Macaulay produced Indians to work and support his country's colonial government in India, Independent India is producing Indians to work for European, American, Australian and Arabic countries. Indians who pass out of their educational institutions, don't give a damn about their own country's development need and their duty towards their mother-land. Their first priority is themselves and their family. Their poor country cannot give them jobs that offer high salaries and high living styles. So they take off to foreign lands. Serving their own country and developing it to the level of advanced countries do not occur to them as a moral duty at all.

Independent India's government did not feel anything wrong in sending India's youth abroad for jobs after spending nearly a crore of rupees of tax payers' money per student whether in medical or engineering or other higher streams of disciplines. Hospitals and factories in India, starving for skilled manpower did not shake the conscience of ministers and bureaucrats in the independent India, because, the lack of development in the country will not affect the well-to-do middle class people since they can afford to import what they lack in their country. It is the 80% lower middle and lower classes who feel the pinches of poor socio-economic development and consequent miseries of living.

If affluent parents find their sons and daughters do not get admission in colleges for lack of seats, they send them abroad to study rather than seeking ways and means to create more seats in India by setting up more colleges. If their children get jobs in government offices and other private and public sector companies, their first preference would be to import foreign technology rather than developing indigenous capacities to substitute imports and become self sufficient in all major branches of science and technology.

Wealthy Indians would deposit their money in foreign banks rather than keep it in India and pay tax to the government. Why should they pay exorbitant tax to the government? They have no qualms about evading tax and depriving their poor country of much needed development funds.

Truly, Macaulay also succeeded in getting Indians believe that one shelf of European literature was more valuable than the entire gamut of Indian literature, as he boldly asserted in 1833, by using education both as a medium and as a message for converting Indians to his points of views. We, of the independent India have failed to use education as a medium as well as a message to reconstruct India, that is Bharat, in accordance with the Mission Statements of the Republic of India, contained in the Preamble to the Constitution of India.

Indian Vedas and Upanishads are no more philosophical and metaphysical literature but Hindu literature to the Indians of Independent India and it cannot be valid or superior to the European or Western literature, to them! Thus, Hinduism as the art and science of evolution has been lost to the people of the emergent republican India. Education in ancient India used to be a set of disciplines for managing the evolution of people towards successful living as a community.

The word 'education' which has its root in Latin word *educare* means 'to bring up,' signifying the fact that education is a process of bringing up individuals for meaningful and useful community life, imparting wisdom of higher truths of the origin of cosmos, its laws and their influence on human evolution and daily living; understanding of the nature of individual being; knowledge of various skills including engineering, architecture, carpentry, life sciences, modern and traditional medical practices like Ayurveda, siddha, yoga and naturopathy; astronomy and astrology; grammar and logic and moral and ethical laws relating to individual evolution and community development.

That Indians have not taken up education for citizenship training and character building as demanded by the Mission Statements in the Preamble to the Constitution of India in right earnestness, right from the beginning of post-Independence period till now, indicates that the education imparted under Lord Macaulay to Europeanize Indians in their thinking had yielded results manifold. When a society is trained to forget its national character and pay allegiance to an alien people in the role of a courtesan, it indeed has not only lost its national character but it also remains as a slave to the aliens. But, when the courtesan is freed to follow her own free will, if she still remains a courtesan, it is then evident that she wallows in her own moral turpitude! Indians, especially the middle class, is in this courtesan's position at present.

Education in India is the most fertile ground for the seeds of corruption to germinate and flourish. Right from the nursery class admissions to the engineering and medical admissions, crores of rupees change coffers and along with changed coffers not only children are initiated into the nuances of un-ethical practices, but their parents are also motivated to try their expertise in unfair and un-ethical practices in other institutions as well,

With education being pandered to the whims of feudal forces in the society, in the forms of separate category of government and municipality run schools for the poor and lower middle class, lower public schools for the middle class, medium public schools for the upper middle class and upper public schools for the upper class rich, the promise of justice, liberty, equality and fraternity made in the Constitution of India, has received a crushing blow. And along with the groaning resulted from that blow, roaring of corruption reverberate in the entire length and breadth of the country that is Bharat!

We Failed to PROMOTE FRATERNITY Among All Citizens of India, Assuring the Dignity of the Individual and the Unity and Integrity of the Nation

The Mission Statements of the Republic of India as contained in the Preamble to the Constitution of India demanded three supreme actions from the citizens of India. **One,** *to constitute India into a sovereign, socialist, secular democratic republic.* **Two,** *to secure to all its citizens: Justice, economic, social and political; Liberty of thought, expression, belief, faith and worship; and Equality of status and of opportunity.* **Three**, *to Promote among all citizens Fraternity, assuring the dignity of the individual and the unity and integrity of the nation.(Emphasis by the author)*

We have already discussed the first two. The third one we are about to discuss, is more important than the first two because, without a sense of fraternity in the society, we may not enjoy the fruits of the first two. Moreover, the goal of the law of evolution at human level is the reign of fraternity i.e. brotherhood at universal level.

However, during the last 62 years after we the people made this resolution in the Preamble to the Constitution of India, there is very little evidence to show that we have promoted **fraternity** among the citizens of India. If we had promoted fraternity, we would have achieved the goals of the first two Mission Statements of the Indian Republic. Ours would have been a enviously progressive and emulative story for the entire world—a happy, healthy, prosperous and peaceful society, had we been promoting **fraternity** among our fellow citizens.

All administrative as well as development policies of the government of India should reflect genuine interest of the government in promoting *fraternity* among the citizens, as demanded in the Preamble to the Constitution of India. That the government of India have failed in this respect is clear from the conflicts raging among the different social, religious and regional groups at the present time. Naxals or Maoists operating in almost all Indian states and the ethnic and liberation movements in North Eastern states and Kashmir are examples of social groups un-integrated with the mainstream India due to the Indian government's disregard to the fundamental mandate given to it by the Constitution to promote **fraternity** among the citizens of India.

A great hurdle for the Indian society in building **fraternity** among themselves is the British model of administration, judiciary and police that the founding fathers have retained even after the British have left India. The reason of course for them to do so was that almost all of them except, perhaps Nehru, was in awe of the efficacious law and order management of the erstwhile British government. We have already read what K.M Munshi, the nominated member of the Constituent Assembly of India had said in justification of retaining the British systems of governance for running the republican India.

We have read also what Dr. Man Mohan Singh, India's Prime Minister had said before the august gathering assembled at Oxford University auditorium to facilitate him on his receiving a honorary degree, in praise of the law and order management of the British government in India. That the British government had run its colonial administrative, judiciary and police forces efficiently so that it could maximize its revenue and consumer interests for its products in India is a well known fact. But, not to see the brutal crushing effects on the Indian masses and the loss of their self respect inflicted by the colonial government is something that can be explained only by the fact that a section of Indians never thought England had colonized their land and deprived their freedom. This section always was on the side of the rulers.

The British ran a feudal government in India to subjugate Indians and harvest natural resources and liquid cash in the form of taxes. For that, it had to nurture a very efficient administration, judiciary and police and other infrastructure. By retaining the governance systems used by the British government in India, in effect the Republic of India ended up with inheriting and nurturing the same feudal governance systems. It is very clear now that the people who perceive the efficacy of the governance systems used by the British government in India, are by the law of association, of feudal mental makeup.

Their recognition of democracy and republicanism is limited only to elected representation of people in running governments. They really do not commit themselves to the principles of justice, liberty, equality and **fraternity** mandated in the Constitution of India. If they had committed themselves to these principles, they would not have continued to cherish and nurture the British feudal governance machineries to run the Republic of India.

I know, we all are parts of this hypocritical mental makeups. Though as Indians, we preach about the virtues of the great Indian Sanadhan Dharma which rests on the *advaita* tenet that the Creator and the created creatures are one and on the resultant universal brotherhood, many of us cannot get rid of the effects of *chatur varna* practices of our forefathers. Feudal mentality is a built in feature of *chatur varna* design, and that takes time to die out!

But, since this book is about the idea of being Indians and the making of India and since that idea comes from the Mission Statements of the Indian Republic given in the Preamble to the Constitution of India, we have to subject the Mission Statements of the Indian Republic for deeper and purposeful understanding.

It was Jawaharlal Nehru who moved the resolution containing these Mission Statements, in the Constituent Assembly in 1946, for drafting a Constitution for India. In a book edited by Dorothy Norman describing Nehru's political evolution, with his own writings and speeches, we get a glimpse of what view Nehru had on the British rule in India. The book published in 1965 had a foreword by Nehru himself. Therefore, we can surmise that what he said in 1936 in his autobiography was valued by him till his death in 1964.

"The British conception of ruling India was the police conception of the State. Government's job was to protect the State and leave the rest to others. Their public finance dealt with military expenditure, police, civil administration, interest on debt. The economic needs of the citizens were not looked after and were sacrificed to British interests. The cultural and other needs of the people, except for a tiny handful, were entirely neglected. The changing conceptions of public finance which brought free and universal education, improvement of public health, care of poor and feeble-minded, insurance of workers against illness, old age, unemployment etc, in other countries, were almost entirely beyond the ken of the Government. It could not indulge in these spending activities, for its tax system was most regressive, taking a much larger proportion of small incomes than of the larger ones and its expenditure on its protective and administrative functions was terribly heavy and swallowed up most of the revenue.

The outstanding feature of British rule was their concentration on everything that went to strengthen their political and economic hold on the country. Everything else was incidental. If they built up a powerful central government and an efficient police force, that people can hardly congratulate themselves on it. Unity is a good thing but unity in subjection is hardly a thing to be proud of. The very strength of a despotic government may become a greater burden for a people; and a police force no doubt, useful in many ways, can be, and has been often enough turned against the very people it is supposed to protect." I am using Nehru's observation of the British rule liberally, because, there is a relevance projecting out of this passage which many readers may find quite applicable to our times and situations in India.

Those who are crediting with good governance to colonial British government might like to see what Nehru said about such good governance: "There have been big changes in India also, and the country is very different from what it was in the eighteenth century—railways, irrigation works, factories, schools and colleges, huge government offices, etc., etc . . . And yet, in spite of these changes, what is India like today? A servile state, with its splendid strength caged up, hardly daring to breathe freely, governed by strangers from afar; her people poor beyond compare, short-lived and incapable of resisting disease and epidemic; illiteracy rampant; vast areas devoid of all sanitary or medical provision; unemployment on a prodigious scale, both among the middle classes and the masses." Things are not much different even now!

Those who praise the efficacy of the British administrative system may see what Nehru said in his autobiography: "Whenever India becomes free and in a position to build her new life as she wants to, she will necessarily require the best of her sons and daughters for this purpose. Good human material is always rare, and in India it is rarer still because of our lack of opportunities under British rule . . . . But of one thing I am quite sure: that no new order can be built up in India so long as the spirit of the Indian Civil Service pervades our administration and our public services. It will either succeed in crushing freedom or will be swept away itself. Only with one type of state is it likely to fit in and that is the fascist type." This eloquent statement by Nehru, though prompts us to congratulate him for it, will also force us to ask him why he did not change the spirit of the Indian Administrative Service (IAS) during his tenure as the Prime Minister. The reasons why he had not changed the spirit of the IAS which followed in the foot steps of the erstwhile ICS are the same which forced the continuance of the British governance systems.

We should remember that the administrative service which Nehru called fascist is the root cause of all our problems in the independent India of ours! Since our criminal and civil procedure codes were written by the British master mind, Lord Macaulay, to bolster the feudal and fascist administration, the judiciary also play fiddle to the fascist administration going on in India. Lord Macaulay (1800-1859), the architect of the Indian Penal Code, wrote that the penal code "should be framed on two great principles,—the principle of suppressing crime with the smallest possible amount of suffering, and the principle of ascertaining truth at the smallest possible cost of time and money" (Trevelyan 1978 (1876): 382).

For the feudal, fascist government of the East India Company in India, Macaulay wrote the penal codes during 1934-1938 when he was in India as a member of the Supreme Council of India assisting Lord William Bentinck, the then Governor General. But the codes were put into practice only after1858 when Britain took direct control of the government from East India Company in the aftermath of India's first freedom struggle in 1857. At first glance, we might feel that Lord Macaulay's statement is a gospel truth. But, if we look for its relevance to the Indian Republic, we might find that his statement has become obsolete because, he had made his statements after observing the needs of the feudal and fascist government to continue in un-hindered power by controlling a feudal society by and large. He was a staunch supporter of the East India Company's government in **India and had convinced the British Parliament not to take over charge from it as yet when some members of the British Parliament urged the government to rule India directly in 1833.**

For democratic and republican governments, the needs of penal codes are primarily for the reformation or for aiding the evolution of every member of the society under their charge through the control and elimination of crimes. Jurisprudence or the philosophy and social relevance of laws for a republican government should be different and will not be same as those of feudal and fascist governments.

All criminal and civil procedure codes of India should have been rewritten after India became a Republic in 1950 keeping in perspective, the Mission Statements of the Republic encoded in the Preamble to the Constitution of India. Economic, social and political justice; liberty of thought, expression, belief, faith and worship; equality of status and opportunities; and promoting fraternity among all citizens assuring the dignity of individuals and unity and integrity of the nation are the mandates for the government of India, and many penal codes framed in British period are counter productive to these mandates. Many offences in feudal regime are not offences in the republican regime. The idea of crime and perception of truth made into statutes by a feudal government will by necessity be different under a democratic republican government.

Especially for promoting fraternity among the citizens of India without caste, creed, or class, our police, lawyers and courts have become a major hindrance in the Republic of India only because we are following the penal codes framed under British feudal governance. If police are not people friendly and only pro-establishment, if an under-trial citizen has to be in jail for years before his charges are framed, and if a case can drag on in the court for 30 years or more, how could we expect fraternity and social harmony in the society?

According to the Mission Statements of Indian Republic given in the Preamble to the Constitution of India, conflicts among the citizens should be resolved peacefully between the offender and the sufferer. Then only fraternity can be maintained in the society. Whether it is the police or the court or even the panchayat or any other citizen-committee, the objective of conflict resolution must be promotion of fraternity in the society as demanded by the Constitution.

A news report in FirstPost.com dated June 29, 2012 by Manoj Kumar showed that villagers can manage their conflicts and crimes amicably among themselves without the intervention of police or courts. In south Bihar, a village called Padia had not known its residents visiting police stations for the past 100 years according to the news report.

Not that the residents have no occasions to fight and injure in moments of anger and anguish. They do, but they always go to the village council of elders for justice and peace which they have been getting from it for generations.

The story is interesting when official statistics indicate that in Bihar about 1.6 million cases are pending with a huge number of cases delayed for more than two decades. There are other villages with similar stories of conflict resolution by village leaders in different parts of India which are unreported in media. With the mandates that we have in the Preamble to the Constitution of India, these models of conflict resolution by village councils and prominent leaders, are quite emulative and unavoidable if we have to promote fraternity as the Constitution of India requires us to do.

Readers are familiar with news stories depicting police stations in India being vicious dens of rapes and custodial torture and deaths. According to a recent report released by Delhi based Asian Centre for Human Rights(ACHR), four deaths occurs daily inside the police stations or jails in India. The Data gathered by ACHR from the National Human Rights Commission (NHRC), revealed that 14231 deaths occurred in judicial custody in police stations and jails during the ten-year period from 2001. All the Indian States are partners in this crime against the Republic of India. It is on record that many tribal area bound Naxal activities had origin in police atrocities committed on people including rapes of women.

This behavior of police coupled with the delay in settlement of cases as long as 30 years or more in Indian courts, had not only generated hatred and revengeful attitudes among families and groups of Indian citizens, but also had gone diametrically opposite to the mandate in the Constitution to promote **fraternity.** An independent and proactive judiciary could not do anything to arrest the decadence of its decorated columns only because their foundations were in the fascism of British governance systems.

SUMMING UP

The Republic of India had declared three Mission Statements in the form of the Preamble to the Constitution of India. They are:

1. To constitute India into a sovereign socialist, secular, democratic republic.
2. To secure to all its citizens: Justice, social, economic and political; Liberty of thought, expression, belief, faith and worship; and Equality of status and opportunity.
3. To promote Fraternity among all citizens assuring the dignity of the individual and the unity and integrity of the nation.

The translation of these grand objectives of the Republic would have made India a healthy, prosperous and peaceful nation at 100% population level. Why this has not happened was because of two major reasons. The first reason was that the founding fathers of the Republic, after making a grand set of objectives for the Republic, as given in the Preamble to the Constitution, somehow failed to live up to these objectives through the many Articles forming the full body of the Constitution. While making Right to

Life a fundamental right, right to housing, food, health, education, income security etc without which Right to Life becomes meaningless, have been kept outside the scope of fundamental right.

The second reason was that instead of creating new republican structures for economic development, administration, judiciary and police at grass root level, the founding fathers opted for the highly centralized and fascist-feudal British systems of administration, judiciary and police for running the Indian Republic. This, in actual fact, has resulted in the Republic being accorded a duplicate British-India status. This harnessing of the fascist-feudal horses to the republican cart by our founding fathers was a perplexing paradox, which no political theorists and Constitutional jurists dared to question or challenge.

The British government ruled India for collecting natural resources and revenue. It never had national and people development in its agenda of governance. Whatever infrastructural development it did for India was incidental to the smooth colonial administration. For that, it had to maintain strong administrative, judicial and police forces in the vast country that is India. The CAG was there for maximizing the revenue collection and minimizing the expenditure. There was no counterpart structure for socio-economic development. There was Public Service Commission for regulating the selection and promotion of staff that supported a revenue collection government. But there was no Private Service Commission for regulating and promoting interests of workers in the organized and unorganized private sector which forms 95% of the work force of the country. Because, for Britain, its government in India was India itself.

Government of the Republic of India followed the British pattern. The result was that the government of India started treating itself as India. It spends 80% of the revenue on itself. Out of the remaining 20%, a good part goes to the middlemen. The state governments also follow suit. The result is that 80% of the population of India did not get the benefits of the development that India had carried out so far in the last 65 years after it became a free nation. All the development benefits were cornered by the middle class which forms about 20% of the Indian society.

India has one of the poorest records in health, education and standard of living in the world. Its rank is 136 among 187 nations in respect of Human Development Index, a yardstick used by UNDP for tracking the socio-economic development made by its member nations.

Indian Republic's Mission Statement mandating both the government and people to promote **Fraternity** among citizens assuring the dignity of individuals and the unity and integrity of the nation was totally neglected till now. On one side, because of the low wage structure and income level, which is even lower than sub-Sahara nations, crime level is on the increase in the form of Naxal militancy, conflicts between social groups due to excessive migration of workers from village to cities, and fights on parochial and linguistic issues between people from underdeveloped states in the North East and industrial towns like Bombay, Bangalore etc.

On the other, delays in settling disputes between citizens by courts for years and decades, vitiate the already low social harmony caused by the economic disparity between the rich and the poor. It is a well known feature of the Indian judicial system that monetary temptations motivate the police, lawyers and even judges to drag on for years and during the pendency of the cases in courts, animosities between offenders, victims, police, lawyers and their related circle of friends and relatives keep growing that even after the judgment of the cases, hatred sways their minds and hearts with tendencies to remain so throughout their lives.

The entire nation had an opportunity to witness the demonstration of 'good governance' inherited by the Indian State from the erstwhile British Government in India, in Delhi in the third week of December, 2012. When news came out about the gang-rape and brutal physical injuries, inflicted by thrusting iron rod into the abdomen of a 23-year old girl student inside a fake passenger bus on December 16, 2012, student activists and supporters gathered in large numbers at the lawns of India Gate and the vicinity of Rashtrapati Bhavan asking for justice to the victim and safer life for women in India on the following three days. The police came and dispersed the crowd using their batons wantonly on peaceful demonstrators from head to foot, drenching them with water cannons and trouncing them with tear gas. The reason given by the police and the Government was that crowd was not allowed in the high security area of the city which was preparing for the Republic Day parade.

The television channels brought the high-handedness of the police to every nook and corner of India and the explanation of the Government for its crude action was not accepted by the nation, because, through the public protest rally what the women of India were conveying to the Government and the society at large was that the situation where every twenty minutes a woman was being raped in India but the rapists were freely moving around, should change and fast with stringent punishments meted out to the culprits.

The Government was forced to move fast in arresting the culprits involved in the gang-rape of the 23-year girl student and help the victim with costly medical aid in India and in Singapore. Though the girl died in Singapore, her suffering and death did not go in vain. The Government ordered establishment of fast-track courts in all the Indian states for dealing with crimes against women and appointed two Commissions to look into the possibility of introducing effective deterrent laws against rapes. All these happened in two weeks.

What is important to note here is the fact that the Government of India, modeled on the colonial British Government's feudal-fascist administration did not have anything in the rule-book to deal peaceably with a crowd of people informing the Government to improve itself. Because, the feudal-fascist administration was designed to treat the Government as the nation and therefore all the rules were to protect the Government, not the people. Elected representatives in the republican Government find it hugely convenient to run such an administration for personal reasons, but, when facing serious public issues, find themselves handicapped for suitable democratic methods for settling those issues.

We are a people without self respect and self esteem. Lord Babington Macaulay had seen to it that Indians forget their civilizational moorings and look up to the Western countries for inner light. The result is that we are a nation of labor suppliers to the more developed Western countries and other Arab nations. Our best of minds are limited to receiving awards from government bodies.

Our people have no fellow feeling and love left in them. If people lie on roads injured, no one will come to their aid and let them die without receiving any medical help. Thousands of our citizens are in jails of foreign countries, but our government does not show any interest to bring them back. We have seen how the Italian government moving the pillars and posts to free their two soldiers who were in Indian jails for killing two of our fishermen.

The low HDI of 136 among 187 nations, is a label for India to be treated by other nations like an irresponsible householder who spends all wealth on himself and put his family members through starvation and untimely death. All our wealth goes to the upkeep of the government and the people who run it. We are a nation clamoring for more military might and front rank in the space race but, we have no compunction for the majority of our people living in poverty.

We, Indians have to find out what is the correct idea of being a true Indian and the making of India. If we attempt for it sooner the better.

Chapter Three

The Idea of Being Indians

If you wanted to know what others in this vast world thought about Indians and surfed the Internet, you must have had the shock of your life when you found that, the name, 'Indians' are mostly referred to the natives of Americas. Nothing to worry! It only meant that information contents on the Net about American Indians are more than those about the inhabitants of the land of Gandhi and Nehru, Bharat. When you know the reason why Christopher Columbus christened the natives of Americas as Indians, you have no reasons either to become chirpy!

Columbus had sailed towards East with financial help from Queen Isabella of Spain, in search of India, the land of spices, silks, exotic fauna and heathens and pagans whom the queen could convert to Christianity. When he landed in Americas on October 12, 1492, he thought actually he landed in India and since he had not seen the real Indians, he mistook the natives, the Mayans, for Indians and referred to them so in his reports back to the Christian Europe. Christian Europeans who later populated Americas not only called natives as Indians, but treated them as unworthy of coexistence with them. Today, the native Americans call themselves Indians.

We know now that the people who came from different lands and ruled India, that is Bharat also had the same view that Indians were pagans and heathens. Especially, Lord Macaulay, on behalf of the British people held that view and tried to 'civilize' Indians to the level of Europeans through education rather than proselytization. Unlike the native Americans, who lost their civilizational moorings at the hands of the plundering Christian zealots from Europe, we in India were lucky enough to have received an opportunity to strengthen the civilizational moorings of our collective being which was weakened by the Christian Britain's plundering. That opportunity was the independence of India.

We have seen in the previous chapter, how we in India were influenced by the education system as well as the penal codes introduced by Macaulay on behalf of the British government. These two had been used by the colonial government of Britain as communication systems capable of molding the middle class Indians in favor of retaining the feudal and fascist governance systems of the colonial government for running the Republic of India. By doing so, we the people of India have not been able to use our independence to our advantage. In this chapter, we will explore the means of using our independence and republican stature for redesigning our autonomous evolution towards a healthy, prosperous and peaceful Indian (Bharatiya) society.

CONSTITUTION OF INDIA CONTAINS THE IDEA OF BEING INDIANS AND A HEALTHY, PROSPEROUS AND PEACEFUL INDIAN SOCIETY

I was born in Kerala, worked in Mumbai and Delhi and am back in Kerala. Similarly, you belong to one of the 28 Indian States or one of the 7 Union Territories. My mother tongue is Malayalam and in your case it may be any one of the 438 living languages of India. Yes, there are 438 spoken languages though only 22 are the scheduled languages of India. I am a Christian and you may belong to any one of the major world religions which are in India.

Well, I have no caste affiliation as I was born into a traditional Christian family which traces its ancestry to the period of St Thomas who established Christian Faith in Kerala in 52AD. But, in your case, it may be that you belong to any one of the major 3000 castes or their sub-castes numbering around 25,000 existing in India or even may be that you are a lucky educated member of one of the 365 scheduled tribes of India. If I may broaden the identity catalogue a bit further, before state re-organization in 1956, my birth-state was Travancore to which Cochin and Malabar were added to make Kerala. And of course, you or your parents were born in any one of the 565 princely states which existed before Independence or the provinces ruled by England directly.

In this vast diverse mosaic I have prepared, what is common to all of us? It is the idea of being Indian! And what contributed to this idea of being Indian in all of us? The answer is, the civilizational flame simmering in our hearts which has been rekindled by the Constitution of India. Simmering, because, the nearly a thousand-year presence of alien civilizations had weakened it but had not snuffed it out like the Mayan experience in the Americas.

I will explain it with an example. You have heard about the Sabarimala Temple where millions of Indians, especially from southern states, go on pilgrimage every year. At the entrance to the sanctum an inscription in both Malayalam and Sanskrit greets the pilgrims. The inscription reads: *Tatvamasi*. This compound word is a combination of three words: *Tat(that) tvam(you) asi(are)*, meaning, *you are that*. Inside the sanctum sanctorum is the deity Ayyappan, who is the son born to Vishnu as Mohini, fathered by Shiva. The sanctorum is placed at a level which is reached by climbing 18 steps through a narrow staircase.

Symbolically, Sabarimala pilgrimage is the journey of every individual through the earthly evolutionary lifetimes. The eighteen steps signify the soul's journey through the eighteen stages consisting of seven solar planes in which our solar system is on the seventh, the seven subtle planes of our solar system whose substances make the seven layered human body and then the four stages a soul has to traverse after reaching the human stage on the ladder of evolution. These four stages are the second birth or the stage when an individual recognizes that he or she and the Creator are one; the stage acquiring the power and purity for receiving communications from higher beings of the spirit world; the stage when he or she can become totally detached with this world's attractions; and the fourth stage when the individual need not take earthly incarnation any more. Since the pilgrims have to compulsorily visit the Muslim mosque at the foot of the hill and pay their respects and obeisance at the tomb of Vavar, a saint believed to have helped Ayyappan to vanquish Mahishasuri, the cruel tormentor of people in the region, before trekking to the hill-top temple, the Sabarimala pilgrimage is also a symbol of communal harmony. Sri Sankaracharya, who revived Hinduism across the length and breadth of Bharat, that is India, is believed to be the initiator of Sabarimala pilgrimage. By the time Sri Sankaracharya was born in Kerala around 800AD, Kerala had already welcomed Islam through traders from Arabia who were close to the Prophet.

Sankaracharya's doctrine of *advaita* which held that the created world and its Creator are one, was the core message of the entire Veda and Upanishads and also the Buddhist religion that had flourished throughout India till Sankaracharya revived Hinduism. The small and bigger kingdoms which occupied the civilizational space of Buddhism and Hinduism or India, were more or less following an ethical code for ruling, based on the oneness of humanity advocated by *advaita*. They had the equitable governance model based on the *Ramarajya* doctrine before them, though, many gave only lip-service to it.

Tat tvam asi appears in Chandogya Upanishad, which explains with lucid examples how the essence of the Supreme Intelligence, the Creator of the Universe, is the essence that animates the human being. *Advaita* is the basis of *Ramarajya* model of governance Lord Rama had practiced in his kingdom. Chandogya Upanishad has also a chapter on Lord Sanat Kumara, a highly evolved being from Venus, advising Maharishi Narada on the power of breath, as the *Brahman,* the Supreme Being. According to the monastic teachings of the Indo-Tibetan mysticism which pans both Buddhism and Hinduism, this being, the highest Initiate of the planet Venus and his associates, had a major role in introducing teachings to humans to save themselves from Karmic destruction which was imminent at some earlier stage in the evolution of Earth. People on Venus are gods compared to us on Earth in respect of evolution, according to these teachings.

What is important for us to note is that, it is this fact of life that the Creator and the created men and women are of same essence and its evolutionary laws, which is at the core of all religions of the world and also at the base of group or national level good governance practiced by priest kings, divine kings, people-elected monarchs and all sorts of democratic and republican governments through-out the history of humankind. When you read the Declaration of Independence made by the leaders of the American Revolution, please note the words carefully: *"we hold these truths self evident that all men are created equal, that they are endowed by their Creator with certain unalienable rights, that among these are Life, Liberty, and the Pursuit of Happiness—That to secure these rights, Governments are instituted among men, deriving their power from the consent of the governed, . . ."* There is a reflection of *advaita* doctrine in the Declaration of Independence because, men who fought for freedom from British government and wrote the Declaration of Independence were members of mystical organizations such as Free Masons, Rosicrucians or similar sects whose fundamental beliefs were based on the *advaita* or *tatvamasi* tenets. Both French Revolution and Indian freedom movement had the thrust given by leaders who were members of mystical organizations or mystically inclined.

While the influence of mystic renaissance writers on American and French Revolutions are well documented and available in textbooks, it is rarely known that Indian freedom movement was also influenced by members and sympathizers of mystic organizations such as the Theosophical Society and Free Masons. In fact the very Indian National Congress which is synonymous to Indian freedom movement was started in 1885 by Theosophists, including Allan Octavian Hume, the British civil servant. Even Nehru and Gandhiji had been influenced by Theosophical teachings as we can understand from their autobiographies. Many Free Masons were functionaries of Indian National Congress. Besides these Western mystical organizations mentioned above, a number of Indian mystical organizations associated with traditional Yoga and Vendanta meditations such as Arya Samaj, Brahmo Samaj and Sri Aurobindo followers also had influenced the freedom movement through their members.

In fact, if we observe the freedom movements of nations across the globe, what we would see is a pattern of heightened desire for freedom on the part of people at large from oppressing rulers caused by a rising tide of spiritual evolution. The Indian spiritual tradition derived from the *advaita* philosophy, rooted in Upanishads and Vedas, had received a boost during the time of freedom struggle and the vision of that struggle was captured in the Constitution of India, in the form of its Preamble. The *Ramarajya* concept derived from *advaita* doctrine is the same which animates the republican concept. And just like no government in the ancient or recent past had been able to translate the *Ramarajya* concept into experiential comforts for people at total population level, our Constitution which carries the *advaita* or *Ramarajya* concept, also could not be translated into real experience for people at total level of the Indian society.

But, unlike in north India, every year the *Ramarajya* concept is brought back to people's memory in Kerala through the celebration and ritualistic practices of Onam, falling every year in end of August or early September, inaugurating the harvest season in that part of the country. Onam is a ten-day festival associated with the annual visit of King Mahabali from the spirit world. According to the legend relating to this festival, King Mahabali's rule was so perfect that people of his kingdom, Malayalees, had no woes or worries and lived in peace and happiness as is promised in *Ramarajya* concept. This had alerted gods in heaven and they complained to Lord Vishnu about it. After all, earth is earth and cannot be heaven, they wanted King Mahabali taught a lesson for crossing his earthly boundary.

Lord Vishnu came to King Mahabali in the guise of a dwarf brahmin and asked for a piece of land measuring three feet just enough for laying down his diminutive body after death. Mahabali graciously allowed the dwarf brahmin to select a suitable place in his kingdom according to his own choice. Upon getting this permission, Lord Vishnu assumed his real divine form and measured earth and heaven in two feet and for the third feet there was no space left for the Lord to place his foot. The ever benevolent Mahabali bent down and showed his own head and the Lord kept His foot on Mahabali's head. As Mahabali was sinking to the nether world, *pathaal*, he had only one wish, that he be allowed to visit his beloved subjects once every year which was granted by Lord Vishnu.

The cultural construct of Mahabali associated with Onam is specific to Malayalees and is used yearly to build up a *Ramarajya* consciousness among them and the ruling hierarchy whether of monarchy of the earlier periods or the democratic government at present. Due to the fact that Muslims and Christians in good proportions occupy the cultural space along with the majority community Hindus, it might not have been appropriate to call it a *Ramarajya* festival and therefore it was given the name Onam, by the Malayalees.

I would like to inform my readers that the world is passing through an astrological period which was existing during the American and French Revolutions. You will recall the uprisings in the Arab world since 2010, known as the Arab Spring and Jasmine Revolution causing many countries to change their autocratic and despotic rule for more people friendly regimes. In India too, a call has arisen from some individual opinion makers and NGOs for a second revolution for freedom from corruption and poverty. A voice is heard all around for more powers in the hands of citizens at grass-root village and urban ward levels. Bharat Swabhiman Andolan, India Against Corruption and Swaraj Andolan are the major organizations involved in leading the political corrective action drive in the country.

If you are, by any chance, involved in any of these campaigns or some other initiatives, my suggestion to you is to take up the Mission Statements of our Republic as given in the Preamble to the Constitution of India and work for the realization of them. That is the only salvation for our beloved country, India. Your idea of being Indian and the making of the India of your dream with that idea, is indeed enshrined in the Mission Statements of the Republic of India contained in the Preamble. All you have to do is to carry out the three supreme actions called for in the Mission Statements of our Republic. Before going into it in full detail, let us look at some symbols which you identify yourself with as an Indian.

THE NATIONAL ANTHEM

When you sing the National Anthem, you attune yourself to the people of your country and to your God whose blessings haven been invoked. Our National Anthem was written in Sanskritized Bengali and since all languages in India have close affinity with Sanskrit, people at large understood its meaning. If some of you have not got the full grip with its overall meaning, I am adding here the official English version of it:

> Thou art the ruler of the minds of all people,
> Dispenser of India's destiny.
> Thy name rouses the hearts of Punjab, Sindhu,
> Gujarat and Maratha,
> Of the Dravida and Orissa and Bangla;
> It echoes in the hills of the Vindhyas and Himalayas, mingles in the music of Yamuna and Ganges and is chanted by the waves of the Indian Ocean.
> They pray for thy blessings and sing thy praise.
> The saving of all people waits in thy hand,
> Thou dispenser of India's destiny.
> Victory, victory, victory to thee.

This English translation was made by Rabindranath Tagore himself on 28th February at the Besant Theosophical College, Madanapalle, Andhra Pradesh at the request of the Principal and students of the college. The song, titled Morning Song of India, has five stanzas. The Hindi version of the first stanza was adopted as India's National Anthem on January 24, 1950 by the Constituent Assembly.

The original Bengali song was sung at the Calcutta session of the Indian National Congress on December 27, 1911. In a letter written to one Pulin Behari Sen in 1939, Tagore had stated that a friend of his in the British Government had asked him to write a felicitation song on the occasion of the visit of King George V. Being a nationalist, he had much difficulty in accepting his friend's request, but since he could not disappoint him, he wrote the song in such a way that the friend would feel that he received the song he asked for, and Tagore could rejoice that he wrote a patriotic song of adorations to God, on behalf of his countrymen.

By decreeing victory to the Ruler of the minds of people and Dispenser of India's destiny through the medium of our National Anthem, we confirm and support the idea of being Indians, given in the Preamble to the Constitution of India. Unlike other songs of prayer and invocation of blessings, our National Anthem enables us to use the power of our minds or thoughts in supporting the Evolutionary Law applicable to Indians and their land as Ruler of our minds and dispenser of our destiny. This power comes to us through the fact of our being parts of the Creator who is also the creative process and the created Universe. After all, as we have seen already in the previous chapters, democracy and republic are premised on this Truth that the Creator and the created are one, not two.

As Indians we are already familiar with decrees, or mantras, such as the *gayatri*; *loka samastha sukhino bhavanthu*; *asato ma sat gamaya* . . . and many more. These decrees create enough sub-atomic forces in patterns according to the nature of the thought patterns of the decrees, which sooner or later become the things or situations that we have decreed for, in the material world. Indeed, Gurudev Rabindranath Tagore knew the secret power of decrees and so also some of our leaders who were instrumental in selecting this song as the National Anthem. In fact, the most important aspect of the idea of being Indian is the opportunity a citizen has, to know about his or her mind's constructive power, from the oral and written sources available around him or her in plenty.

NATIONAL FLAG

Have we ever thought that our National Flag is also a source of the idea of our being Indians? I used to stand before the flag and salute as others did on important national occasions without much idea about it except that it was being honored because it was the National Flag. But, when I have started writing this book and hunted for crucial information, I found out that the National Flag is indeed also the symbol of our idea of being Indians. This must be so, because, after adopting the Constitution of India, all essential symbols such as the National Anthem, National Flag and the National Emblem should reflect the core philosophy surrounding the objectives of our Republic enshrined in the Constitution.

Our National Flag was adopted by the Constituent Assembly of India on July 22, 1947, a few days before India became independent. Dr. S. Radhakrishnan, who was a Member of the Constituent Assembly then and who later became India's first Vice President and second President, clarified the adopted flag and described its significance as follows

"Bhagwa or the saffron color denotes renunciation or disinterestedness. Our leaders must be indifferent to material gains and dedicate themselves to their work. The white in the center is light, the path of truth to guide our conduct. The green shows our relation to the earth, our relation to the plant life here, on which all other life depends. The Ashoka Chakra in the center of the white is the wheel of the law of dharma. Truth or satya, dharma or virtue ought to be the controlling principle of those who work under this flag. Again, the wheel denotes motion. There is death in stagnation. There is life in movement. India should no more resist change, it must move and go forward. The wheel represents the dynamism of a peaceful change."

I have shown Dr Radhakrishnan's statement taken from Wikipedia in italics to emphasize how relevant his words are today for the leadership of this country across all political parties and ideological configurations. Since he had contextualized his statements for the leaders who were destined to lead the Republic of India, I would go a little further and give some additional details about the symbolic relevance of our National Flag to all citizens of India. More over, the idea of being Indian also embraces the idea of the National Flag. I am sure many of you are aware that according to the Indo-Tibetan spiritual sciences, Godhead has the three prime colors i.e. blue, yellow and red. Blue represents Will or Life, yellow represents Wisdom or Light and red represents Love or Harmony aspects of the Godhead. We know that saffron or orange color is a combination of red and yellow and therefore it is a union of love and wisdom.

Similarly, green is a combination of blue and yellow and therefore represents life and wisdom. In case of white color, we know that it is a combination of all seven colors. The wheel at the center of the white stripe is in indigo the seventh color, a combination of blue and red representing the cyclic manifestations of life in precise harmony.

Lord Krishna is always portrayed in indigo color wearing a yellow attire representing the triune color of Godhead. From time immemorial, Indigo and yellow are used to represent royalty, the government using the will, love and wisdom in ruling the worldly affairs by men and cosmic affairs by God. Indigo God dressed in yellow is the king of the cosmos and also the self of men and women. Though the indigo God as such, has not been represented in the flag, His virtues have been captured in the colors and graphics of the flag. The wheel especially, represent God as the eternal Law of Evolution which manifests in small and larger cycles. Here we must appreciate the age old concept of re-incarnation or rebirth of souls believed in by Hindus, Buddhists, Jains, Parsis and an assortment of mystical sects, as the law of evolutionary life of people as well as general life-streams. I am aware that many Christians also believe in re-incarnation as the law of life which Jesus talked about as the Law. There are proofs in the Bible showing Jesus and his disciples having knowledge of the law of Karma and Re-incarnation.

But, for us in India, who believe in the involution of the spirit of God on the earth plane and then evolution of this spirit back to Godhood through cycles of births and deaths in different cultures, climes, castes, creeds or religions changing its physical body's gender alternately or according to the need of its evolution in a particular gender, the wheel of life and law is a constant reminder to us of our duty to obey it for moving upward on the ladder of evolution.

It is believed generally that Dr Ambedkar had influenced the members of the Constituent Assembly in selecting the Wheel of Law or the *dharma chakra,* which is also known as the *kaalachakra,* to be added to the National Flag. He did well in doing so. Indians with many religions, castes and linguistic groups and communal and ideological biases, are well advised to give utmost respect to meanings and implications of this *dharma chakra.*

The twenty-four spokes of the wheel in the National Flag represents the 24 yugas or epochs of the three and a half Periods, each consisting of 7 yugas or epochs, the Earth has to pass through before it completes its evolution along with its life-streams. According to the Indo-Tibetan mysticism, the Earth had passed through 3 major Periods and 4 yugas or epochs. The Earth is in the 5th yuga or epoch at present of the 4th Period. The Judaic-Islamic-Christian mysticism of the Old and New Testament Bible also conform to this chronology of Earth's and therefore the humanity's past and future evolution. Prophets Ezekiel and Daniel of Old Testament and St John the Revelator of the New Testament also talked of the three and half Periods the Earth has to traverse in the future. The Earth has completed 25 epochs and we are in the 26th epoch out of the total 49 epochs consisting of the present cycle of manifestation and evolution of the Earth.

Thus, the various symbols of the National Flag, have close correspondence with we, the people of India in our daily lives. The colors of Godhead also represent the five elements or the building blocks of life on Earth. The blue represents Water;

Yellow represents Air; red represents Fire; green represents Earth while white with a tinge of violet represents Ether. Also the *tridosha* or the three imbalances in the Ayurveda such as the *vata, pittha* and *kabha* are the imbalances of Air, Fire and Water respectively with Earth and Ether in the human body.

Finally, the National Flag is a combination of symbols representing various aspects of our daily life. India's National Flag represents another facet of the idea of being Indian.

NATIONAL EMBLEM OF INDIA

The National Emblem of India consists of elements adapted from the Lion Capital of Ashoka and the inscription, 'satyameva jayate' taken from Mundaka Upanishad. The Constituent Assembly adopted this configuration as the National Emblem of India on January 26, 1950, on the day India became a Republic with Constitution of India coming into effect on that day. Why this particular configuration was chosen as our National Emblem? The Lion Capital is the symbolic story of the cyclic evolution of the Earth. And *satyameva jayate* is the affirmative statement of that story.

Emperor Ashoka had spread his edicts and teachings of the Buddha written on pillars, stone surfaces and cave walls throughout his vast empire. The pillars on which the edicts appeared used to be ornate with carved capital blocks of animals at the top. In fact, he had made the images of lion, elephant, horse and bull to adorn the top of these pillars. The Lion Capital atop the Ashoka Pillar installed in Sarnath, near Varanasi in Uttar Pradesh, had distinct elements to represent different aspects of the evolution story of our Earth. First, the

Lion Capital begins at the end of the trunk of the pillar with an inverted bell shaped lotus on whose flatted bottom rests the circular base that bear the four lions standing back to back. The circular base is thick enough to carry carved figures of a lion, a galloping horse, a bull and an elephant.

Originally atop the figures of the four lions, a wheel was fixed in standing position between their necks. This wheel is missing from the Lion Capital that is kept in the museum at Sarnath. The pillar still stands without the Lion Capital in Sarnath where Buddha had started his long mystic career with the famous sermon on dharma.

In mystic symbolism associated with the Indo-Tibetan as well as all ancient civilizations, the lotus has the distinct character of the *swayambhu* or the causeless Cause. This is because, the lotus is self-germinating without the intervention of outside fertilizing agent. Moreover, lotus by occupying earth, water and air or space simultaneously and bloom under sunlight, is reckoned as symbol of cosmos. In this, the earth represents matter, the water represents spirit and the sun-light represents the central Sun from which all manifested worlds have sprung out.

The four animals and the wheel with 24 spokes on the rim side of the circular base and the four lions standing back to back facing the four directions represent the evolution of the Earth. In the Indo-Tibetan and the Western mysticism, the Earth has to pass through seven Periods each of which has seven sub-periods, before it completes its evolution and ascension back to the Godhead. Accordingly, the Earth has already completed three Periods and is in the fifth sub-period of fourth at present. This means, Earth has to go through three main Periods and three sub-periods including the one in which we are at present, before it reaches culmination of evolution. The 24 sub-periods—twenty one periods of the three main Periods and the three sub-periods yet to complete including our present one are represented in the 24-spoked wheel.

The first Period was known as Saturn Period in which the mineral world was evolving. The lion engraved in the circular base represent this first Period. The second Period was known as Sun Period in which the plant life evolved. The horse represent this second Period. The third Period was known as Moon Period and the animal life evolved in this Period. The bull in the circular panel represent this Period. The fourth Period is known as the Earth Period in which human life has begun and is evolving. The elephant represents this Period. In the Earth Period, four sub-periods have already elapsed and the names of them are: Polarian period, Hyperborean period, Lemurian period and the Atlantian period. We are in the Aryan period, the fifth sub-period. The sixth and seventh sub-periods will make the present humanity perfect like Rama of Ayodhya requiring no more rebirth to humans on Earth. Through the fifth Jupiter Period, sixth Venus Period and the seventh Vulcan Period and their 21 sub-periods, today's animal, plant and mineral life streams would have evolved to humans successively.

The four lions of the Lion Capital represent the Earth with its four directions. Atop their heads, there was a wheel with 24 spokes symbolizing the 24 sub-periods the Earth has to traverse for its complete evolution. The Law of cause and effect controls the entire spectrum of evolution across these periods for Earth and its life-streams. In fact, this Law controls the entire spectrum of cosmic manifestations. In humans, this Law controls our evolution through the law of Karma and Reincarnation. Buddha was emphatic on calling our attention to this fact of this Law. Our evolution depended on the love for our fellowmen, fellow-women and fellow-creatures, plants and minerals expressed in the form of non-violence and social service.

Our leaders who selected the inscription 'satyameva jayate,' knew its relevance to the rest of the elements in the configured National Emblem. In fact, 'satyameva jayate' is an affirmation or Amen to the messages conveyed through the Lion Capital of Ashoka. Standing alone, this piece of verse taken from the Mundaka Upanishad will not convey its really intended meaning, unless connected with the full context in which it was recorded. The whole Mundaka Upanishad, divided in 3 books deals with *Brahman* as the source of all created worlds and as the self of all men and women. Knowledge of *Brahman* the Truth is imparted to one Saunaka, a householder by sage Angiras. Stanza No.6 of Book 3 reads:

> *'It is truth that conquers, not falsehood.*
> *By truth is laid out the path to the gods*
> *By which the Rsis, their desires fulfilled,*
> *Travel to the highest abode of truth.'*

The truth of *Brahman* the causeless Cause becoming Earth and its life-streams is depicted in the Lion Capital of Ashoka. The inscription *'satyam eva jayate'* just below the Lion Capital, is an emphatic affirmation of that truth.

National Symbols are Reminders of Our Commitment to Ourselves

The National Anthem, the National Flag and the National Emblem are national symbols and as such, they are not only our physical identities to the external world, but also our spiritual identities of our personality to both external world and to ourselves. We have seen how the National Anthem is our decree of victory to the evolutionary plan of the Creator for us as Indians.

Similarly, we had noted the symbolic significance of our National Flag. Its saffron color as a combination of yellow(wisdom) and red(love), denote perfect personality traits of self-control, self-confidence and social dedication. Its green color as a combination of yellow (wisdom) and blue (life), denote health and prosperity not only of ourselves but also of Mother Earth. Its white color as combinations of all the seven hues, signify oneness among people and oneness of people with the cosmos and the resultant peace. This truth of humanity's oneness with the Creator and the resultant oneness among people through the cycles of deaths, rebirths and civilizational changes is symbolized through the wheel placed at the center of the white stripe. This wheel represent the Law of our evolution through cycles of deaths, rebirths and national and civilizational *pralayas* or destruction and reappearance as new civilizations. The Law demands that a certain minimum set of *karmas* or actions we do as duties or *dharmas* to steer our evolution towards successful living.

We have also seen the real meaning of the inscription 'satyameva jayate' forming part of the National Emblem. Here again, the truth is that we are *Brahman*, the creative intelligence and the creative motion that manifest in and through the world we live in. A careful scrutiny of the Preamble to the Constitution of India will reveal that we have made a covenant with ourselves to enhance our vision and enlarge our personality to make India a great nation out of ourselves. The three national symbols that we have just examined are reminders of our potential to fulfill that covenant.

OUR COVENANT WITH OURSELVES TO MAKE INDIA A GREAT NATION OUT OF OURSELVES

In chapter one, we had a thorough discussion on the syntactic and semantic relevance of the words and phrases used in the Preamble to the Constitution of India as Mission Statements of the Republic of India. In chapter two, we have noted that the Mission Statements of our Republic have failed to materialize due to the impertinent retention of the British governance structures for managing the Republic. In the remaining part of this chapter, we will explore the possibility of discovering the idea of being Indian in the Mission Statements of the Republic, we have made as covenant with ourselves so that we will get a clue to the making of India, out of our idea of being Indian. In chapter four, we will discuss the details of that clue. Perhaps, as Indian citizens we were not taking the Constitution of India very seriously for anything. Nobody has told us that the Constitution of India contains the Mission Statements of the Republic of India and much less that those missions were our commitments to ourselves.

Our first commitment was to constitute India into a sovereign, socialist, secular, democratic republic: Perhaps, here again, we thought that it is the government of the day which will look after this commitment. Government of the day will have to look after this commitment. But, in no less degree of involvement and sincerity, we have also to look after this commitment. Because, we, the people of India have made this commitment to ourselves. *Our second commitment* was to secure to all its (India's) citizens JUSTICE economic, social and political; LIBERTY of thought, expression, belief, faith and worship; EQUALITY of status and opportunity and *our third commitment to ourselves* was to promote FRATERNITY assuring the dignity of the individual and the unity and the integrity of the nation.

The *second* and *third commitments* could have been easier to fulfill, if the *first commitment* was carried out successfully. The *first commitment* could not be carried out successfully, because, we thought by conducting elections and sending our representatives to local, state and central governments, we have constituted India into a sovereign, socialist, secular, democratic republic! Elections, and people-represented local bodies, state legislatures and central parliaments could exist also in capitalist, fascist, authoritarian, totalitarian, autocratic, oligarchic democracies and republics. In various parts of the world, there are elected governments functioning in non-democratic and non-republican manner with any one or all of these just categorized variety of governance style.

Jeffrey A. Winters, columnist, writing in the October/ December, 2011 issue of The American Interest magazine had strongly indicted the US government of being a oligarchic democracy. Quite a few writers have come forward in analyzing the world trends of democracies becoming oligarchic.

Riaz Haq, a south Asia watcher had in his blog, *Haq's Musings* dated July 27, 2011 said that India is the world's biggest oligarchy, by quoting a New York Times story of that date: "India's billionaires control a considerably larger share of the national wealth than do the superrich in bigger economies like those of Germany, Britain and Japan. Among the Indian billionaires included on the most recent Forbes rich list, a majority have derived their wealth from land, natural resources or government contracts and licenses, all areas that require support from politicians."

"Among India's powerful billionaires, the New York Times story particularly features Gautam Adani whose cozy relationship with Gujarat Chief Minister Narendra Modi has made him the tenth richest man in India," wrote Riaz Haq in his blog. The New York Times report said that 'Mr. Adani has benefited from various governmental approvals and also bought coastal land from the Gujarat government at very low prices—in one instance paying as little as $540 an acre. Once he completed infrastructure, Mr. Adani sold land at a handsome profit to corporations locating inside the economic zone, including one parcel to Indian Oil Corporation, a state-owned firm, for $54,000 an acre.'

"The extraordinary power and influence of India's super rich has played out to the detriment of ordinary Indians who make up the world's largest population of poor, hungry, illiterate and sick people. It poses a serious challenge to India's democracy, often claimed as the world's largest, to meet the very basic needs of its people in whose name the rulers supposedly govern the country," wrote the acerbic Asia Watch blogger.

In an article written by Sourav Mitra in Tehelka, the magazine that champions the cause of economic and social justice for people, dated August 10, 2012, India was compared to a pompous emperor:

"If you could get India to don the fabled Emperor's new clothes, you would discover the stark self-deceiving illusions that serve as the foundations of our collective national consciousness:

1. India is not a democracy. It is a conglomerate of feudal oligarchies distributed across the Centre and the states. Despite proud and strident claims of being the largest democracy in the world, India cannot be a democracy. A democracy is a rule of the people, but in India, the multifarious political leaderships seldom hear the people and heed them even less. It is the will of the powerful few that always plays out.

2. India's great diversity is not the driver of our feverishly proclaimed "great unity", nor can it be the source of our much-proclaimed pride. Our great diversity is the seed of our great divisions, antagonisms that often border on hatred, and shame, no matter how fiercely we deny it. India wallows divided by its myriad languages, religions and castes and their respective cultures. The effects are sometimes invisible, sometimes explosive and sometimes somewhere between invisible and explosive.

3. India's world-revered religiosity is not the most magical salvation trick that man ever made up. It is, in fact, an immaculate sham. If not, all our religious sects would not be so tainted with scandals of corruption, crime, misdemeanor, jingoism or terror and this self-proclaimed god-fearing nation would not degenerate into the depraved level of corruption and crime it has." There are so many examples splashed in our national media over the last few years showing that India never was a true sovereign, socialist, secular, democratic republic. You only have to go on the Internet and search to prove this point to yourselves!

We all subscribe to democratic and religious doctrines of most superior and spiritual kinds and yet our national-scape is full of incidents that could happen only in primitive societies. For example, a Kolkata based news report dated September 3, 2012 in Times of India, Delhi, narrated about a middle aged woman who after being thrown out of her husband's house by the drunkard husband, sold her 3 daughters aged 10, 8 and 4 years for just Rs.130 to three couples out of fear that her daughters might become preys to pimps serving the rapacious sex industry. This is not an isolated case. So many such stories appear in newspapers in regular frequency. You and I are ready to help. But how? Our feigned helplessness is proof that we were not educated by our parents and we have not educated our children about what sovereignty, socialism, secularism and democratic republicanism mean to us and our nation.

This conundrum can be explained with some examples: You know very well that India has a very ambitious space program. In 2008 we had a moon probing program by sending Chandrayaan-1 and we will have another moon probe in 2013 by sending Chandrayaan-2. As Prime Minister announced on August 15, 2012 from the ramparts of Red Fort, in Delhi, we will have sent a spacecraft to Mars in November 2013 and the space machine will reach Mar's orbit in 11 months. American space-craft Curiosity had landed on Mars in the first week of August 2012 and is in sound technological health for doing its assigned probe of the Martian surface. We are in the company of the most developed country of the world as far as space technology is concerned. We must have spent about Rs.20,000crore on space program by now.

Another area of India's covetable performance is its defense program. We are already in the nuclear weapon club of seven members who are developed nations except Pakistan. On defence, we are spending nearly 3% of our GDP which is 8,279,976 crore rupees and 3% of this amount is Rs.248399 crores. We have all the latest warfare support systems in navy, air force and army services.

With its commendable performance in science and technology, especially in information technology and subsequent rise in the world economy to stand along with the top ten developed countries of the world, India is reckoned as a rising world power. We all can be proud of that fact. But, somehow India as a nation is somewhat like the proverbial householder who keeps up a bright personal image in front of the public while at home, he is a wayward spendthrift who keeps his family members hungry, undernourished, ill clad and ill healthy.

According to a UN report released in 2010, 60.6 crore people in India did not have access to a toilet facility and defecated in the open spaces. In June 2012, Mr. Jairam Ramesh, India's Rural Development Minister said that India was world's largest open air toilet and that Pakistan, Bangladesh and Afghanistan had better toilet facilities. Surprisingly all households which had toilet facilities in India were not bringing credit to India either.

For instance, in the Supreme Court of India, on September 3, 2012, the NGO Safai Karmachari Andolan, while presenting its case for the eradication of manual scavenging, declared that out of the total 24.6 crore households in India, 26 lakh households had insanitary toilets as 13.14 lakhs toilets discharged excreta directly into open drains while 4.97 lakh dry toilets were serviced by animals like pigs and dogs and 7.94 lakh were cleaned manually by workers belonging to a certain low caste section of the community, carrying the containers on their heads.

While we are conscious of India's economy growing to the 11th rank in size among the world's nations, what we forget is that when considered in terms of per capita GDP, India stands at 141st among the nations of the world with USD. 1389 per annum. The people living below poverty line in India is 32.7% of the population with daily earning of less than USD.1.25. But, people with a daily earning of USD.2 or less, is 68.7% of the population in India. While these are World Bank figures, India's Planning Commission insists that people with earning less than Rs.26 per day in urban areas and Rs.24 per day in rural areas are really poor. While Planning Commission has worked out these figures to bring down the number of people under poverty line, this exercise on Planning Commission's part had exposed the Government's idea about what poverty is and its attitude towards the poor.

In a study released by the London School of Economics in March 2012, the conclusion of participant scholars was that India cannot become a super power. Ramachandra Guha, the reputed historian of the Independent India and author of the book, India After Gandhi, who also was a participant in the LSE study gave cogent reasons for the study's depressing conclusion. Some of the factors that block India from becoming super power were:

- India's insurgency in Kashmir and North East region is not anywhere near a finishing line.
- Naxalite anti-state terror has spread in many states with widening gains on continuous scale.
- Gap between the rich and the poor after the globalization of Indian economy is widening in frightening scale.
- Political parties have become family business in India.
- Environmental degradation is at debilitating scale.
- Media apathy in development reporting and campaigning have diminished as sensation mongering and celebrity promoting consumed them.
- Fundamentalism of religious groups has acquired dominance in political decisions.
- The political fragmentation into so many self seeking parties has incurred an uncertain future for governance.
- All public institutions have become corrupt. And
- All the neighboring nations are also unstable.

Our worry is not that India cannot become a super power. Our worry is that the ten reasons cited by Ramachandra Guha are there and are going to be there for a long time to come only because, we the people of India have failed to monitor the Mission Statements of our Republic as given in the Constitution of India whether they were being implemented or not and if not being implemented, then why not? Who are all responsible for its non-implementation? In fact, I would add the caste factor to the list of R. Guha's list. Because, the caste factor comes directly in opposition to the Constitutional obligation of *promoting fraternity.*

If we look back through the growing years of our Republic, we can see that ignoring to *promote fraternity* was at the root of all major economic, social and political turmoil that we as a society had to go through! Ramachandra Guha would not have had the opportunity to write and lecture the way he did during the last few years and still doing, on the 'ten reasons why India will not become a super power,' if we, the people of India had insisted on fulfilling the *commitment* we made in our Constitution *to promote fraternity*. This was our *third commitment* in the Preamble to the Constitution.

But as I mentioned earlier, our *second commitment*, i.e. '*to secure justice, liberty and equality*' and *third commitment,* i.e. '*to promote fraternity*' would have been easier and possible had we implemented our *first commitment*, i.e. '*to constitute India into a sovereign, socialist, secular democratic republic.*' We have seen in the second chapter that due to the retention of the British colonial apparatus of governance with its inbuilt feudal-fascist motivational drive, was not only ineffective but detrimental to the making of the Republic of India. In our efforts to practice or live the idea of being Indians, we are required to undertake two jobs: one, to promote the Mission Statements of the Indian Republic as contained in the Preamble to the Constitution to promote the idea of being Indian contained therein and two, to replace the British made feudal-fascist governance apparatus with republican governance apparatus.

Once we do these two jobs, India would be a super power in terms of moral and spiritual power having raised its society to its divine heights in health, prosperity and peace at 100% population level. Otherwise, how can we be proud of our achievements in science and technology, space and defence when half of our people are poor, undernourished, under educated, ill clad and insecure in income and social life? If the idea of being Indians is living our lives to our full divine potential and one with our fellowmen and women and one with our Creator, as we ourselves have mandated in the Preamble to our Constitution, and symbolized them in our National Anthem, National Flag and National Emblem, then, we cannot sit idle and be fed with media celebration of growing GDP of India and the number of celebrities and billionaires amongst us.

But, my dear readers, please let us not prolong our lethargy of not living the idea of being true Indians. Come, let us translate the Mission Statements of our Republic jointly and individually. Let us constitute India into a ***sovereign, socialist, secular, democratic republic*** in right earnestness and live the idea of being Indians as contained therein. Let each one of us be a sovereign, socialist, secular and democratic individual and recognize the sovereignty and the socialistic, secularist and democratic nature of the souls of all other citizens around us and their rights arising from those natures.

Writing in the preface of the book, 'Indian Inheritance' edited by S. Ramakrishnan and brought out by Bharatiya Vidya Bhavan in 1951, Dr K.M. Munshi, its founder president wrote: "We seek the dignity of man, which necessarily implies the creation of social conditions which would allow him freedom to evolve along the lines of his own temperament and capacities; we seek the harmony of individual efforts and social relations, not in any makeshift way, but within the framework of the Moral Order; we seek the creative art of life; by the alchemy of which, human limitations are progressively transmuted, so that man may become the instrument of God, and is able to see Him in all and all in Him." Obviously Kulapati Munshi, as he was fondly called by his admirers, was writing about the goals of the Bharatiya Vidya Bhavan.

But as a leading member of the Constituent Assembly of India, a member of the Constitution Drafting Committee under the chairmanship of Dr. B.R. Ambedkar and also as a member of the National Flag Selection Committee, Dr Munshi was very much involved in creating the idea of being Indian of a new independent India. The social conditions and systems he sought to create through Bharatiya Vidya Bhavan, for transmuting human limitations into possibilities of becoming instrument of God and seeing God in all and all in God, were the same he and his fellow members of the Constituent Assembly sought to create through the Preamble to the Constitution of India.

All the *three commitments* made by we, the people of India in the Preamble to the Constitution of India, are reflected in the preface Dr Munshi had written for the book, 'Indian Inheritance.' What Dr Munshi sought to achieve through the preface to the book, was at the core of the *advaita* philosophy, which holds that the Creator had become the created phenomenal world of men and women; that these men and women are on the evolutionary path leading to their divine heights of faculty and personal growth; that their evolution is controlled by the evolutionary law of cause and effect; and that the aim of this evolutionary law is the successful evolution of the total human race toward health, prosperity, peace and happiness. These eternal verities or *sanatana dharma* precepts which form the core of Indian civilization are reflected in the missions of the Indian republic as framed in the Preamble to the Constitution of India. Democracy and republicanism are premised on these eternal verities or *sanatana dharma*.

A reality which almost all of us failed to note was that the concept and design of democratic and republican state, have their origin in the writings and teachings of mystics, social philosophers and leaders who had the insight into the evolutionary laws of the universe rooted in the oneness existed between the humans and their Creator and among the humans themselves. In the West, from the period of Pythagoras, Socrates, Plato and Aristotle, they were members of the ancient and modern mystical organizations such as the Freemasons, Rosicrucians, Theosophists etc and in the East, they were members of the many mystical groups affiliated to Hindu and Buddhist religions.

The governance model, the Republic of India followed should have been the one developed from the *advaita* or *sanatana dharma* concept that animated the three Mission Statements of the Republic appearing in the Preamble to the Constitution of India. In fact, any democratic republican governance model, anywhere in the world, would have the eternal verities or the *sanatana dharma* which is common to both Western and Eastern religions, as their driving spirit. The eternal verities enshrined in the *advaita* or *sanatana* dharma doctrine would boil down to one fiat for the humanity: universal brotherhood. Follow it, flourish and prosper or perish!

The communist republics may not ascribe to a divine source of common origin of mankind, but they cannot deny the origin of the universe from a single source which has the presence of intelligence, harmony and precision throughout its process of becoming the universe. If a communist or an atheist denies this intelligent common source of origin, he or she is denying his or her own being! The causeless Cause, the Supreme Source is the Self of all beings including we, the people of India.

We have already seen in the second chapter, why we the people of India failed to develop a republican governance model out of our Constitution. We have seen that, the founding fathers of our Republic wanted only a self rule or *swaraj* by Indians for India and for that they wanted only the British rulers out, not their systems of governance. In their eyes the British governance in India was emulative and they therefore retained the British made organs of governance for running the Republic of India. The ruling hierarchies and the political parties in the post-Independence India too, held the views of the founding fathers and the result is that Independence of India benefited only 20% of the people who are in or close to the government. The vast majority, constituting 80% of the population of India, has lost the benefit of Indian Independence. They, people in this category, are harboring the desire for a second freedom struggle which some among them call the 'total revolution!' Anna Hazare, Arvind Kejriwal and Swami Ramdev are the key players who cry for a total revolution and all of you are familiar with their ideologies and agenda.

Only time will tell whether they will succeed in making Indians a prosperous and peaceful people. But, I can predict them success only if they concentrate on developing a governance model based on the missions of the Indian Republic contained in the Preamble to the Constitution of India. While developing such governance model, they will have to find a way to replace or remodel the present government structures inherited from British rulers of colonial India.

Tim Sebastian's Outsider program on Bloomberg Tv on September 19, 2012, on 'Is India Ripe for a Revolution,' 60% of the viewers felt India was ripe for a revolution. While the panelists on Tim Sebastian's show discussed the unjust Indian society which pampered the rich to grow more rich and punished the poor to become more poor with each passing day, the reason for such cruel fate for the poor was not correctly diagnosed. It is ironic really, to know that we, the people of India have to wage a second revolution to get rid of the government systems contributed by the British colonial government just because, the founding fathers of the Indian Republic really wanted only the eviction of the British rulers and not their ruling machinery on the culmination of the first revolution that people waged for nearly a hundred years. When Kejriwal talks of a total revolution or *sampoorna kranti,* what he unconsciously wants is the replacement of the fascist British ruling systems inherited by Independent India with the democratic republican governance systems which are yet to be developed. The revolution talked about by eminent people in Tim Sebastian's show is the revolution of dismantling the fascist, feudal government systems of the British rulers inherited by we the people of India, though they could not articulate the how and what of the revolution. They only discussed the why of the revolution that, to them, indicated India was ripe for a revolution.

But a second revolution is not only of dismantling the British government systems adopted by our founding fathers for us, but also of intelligent replacement of them with carefully designed republican government structures of administration, judiciary and police. The second revolution, as the first revolution, should be and would be non-violent and more of persuasive attitudinal change of people. There is a deep belief in the minds of a large number of people in the governments and political parties across the country that, the British government had been providing good governance in India, though, politically Britain was not justified in ruling us.

The responsibility of replacing the British legacy of feudal fascist governance structures with democratic republican governance structures is on us now, my dear readers and fellow citizens of India that is Bharat the land of the epics of *ramayana* and *mahabharata* which provided the moral and ethical ideas to the Indians for several thousands of years. "In fact, the ramayana and mahabharata are the two encyclopedias of the ancient Aryan life and wisdom, portraying an ideal civilization, which humanity has yet to aspire after," wrote Jawaharlal Nehru, concluding his brief portrayals of these two epics in the book, 'Indian Inheritance,' published by Bharatiya Vidya Bhavan, in 1951.

The idea of being Indians nurtured by the aspirations of Indians over the centuries for an ideal civilization, as depicted in our epics, is recaptured in the missions of the Indian Republic, enshrined in the Preamble to the Constitution of India for pushing us towards the realization of the ideal civilization Indians aspired for over the past many centuries, nay, many millennia. Today, on a collective basis human race has reached a far more advanced stage in its evolution than that of the humanity of the epic period and the republican democratic state is proof enough of that fact and the state is capable of taking care of the all round evolution of people at collective level across the nations of the world. The missions of the Indian Republic as narrated in the Preamble to the Constitution of India are indeed the design parameters for aiding the collective all round evolution of Indians.

Based on the missions of the Republic of India, as appearing in the Preamble to the Constitution of India, we must develop our governance model for running the Republic of India. A 12-commission governance model is being presented here for your scrutiny and approval and if you are convinced of its merits in terms of its being able to manage the collective all round evolution of our citizens at total level of the Indian society, then discuss about it with your family, friends and peers. I call it, the *sarvodaya model of good governance*. It facilitates self-governance at personal level and state governance at collective level.

Before going any further, let us remember the fact that the missions of the Republic of India as given in the Preamble to the Constitution of India have not been fully and functionally structuralized for a democratic and republican socio-economic-cultural life for the Indian society as a whole and that is the reason why we are emboldened to venture into the exercise of devising a possible good governance model. We must remember at this juncture that the clamor for a total revolution or for a second revolution among the majority of the people of India is due to the aforesaid fact that the missions of the Republic of India as stated in the Preamble to the Constitution of India were not translated effectively neither in the elongated body-texts of the Constitution nor in the governance machineries engaged by the governments at the federal, state and local levels.

We must also remember that any good governance model adopted for administering a democratic republic, needs to be directed towards helping the citizens for self-governance or management of their personal evolution towards successful self development at physical, mental and spiritual levels, while being able to organize the state machineries to coordinate all socio-economic-cultural and natural institutions for aiding the successful evolution of citizens at total level of the society. The *sarvodaya model of good governance* has been developed with these twin needs of a good governance model in view

SARVODAYA MODEL OF GOOD GOVERNANCE AND ITS TWELVE COMMISSIONS

The word, 'sarvodaya' has been adopted by me because of its ability to represent the concept of *advaita* on which democracy and republican doctrines are premised and which symbolizes the law of evolution as the process of cause and effect on human race at individual and collective levels. Gandhiji, gave the name *sarvodaya* to his philosophy of life, after reading John Ruskin's book, UNTO THIS LAST which dealt with the principles of Christian economic socialism. John Ruskin had based the theme of his book on a parable of Jesus quoted in the Bible. Jesus used the parable of a rich farmer and a bunch of workers who were hired on the same day but at different times of the day and paid the same wage irrespective of their short and longer durations of work done, implying that workers have same needs of running their families and they need to be paid according to their needs and the labor of workers should be valued on the basis of their need to provide their families with equitable level of standard of living. Gandhiji wanted an equitable wage system in India for the workers according to their needs and he diagnosed that the pay for an advocate and a craftsman should not be much unequal as both have almost same family needs of comforts.

Jesus narrated the parable of the rich farmer and workers to substantiate the validity of what he said earlier to his disciples that it was difficult for the rich to get to heaven, but however, for the Father in heaven everything was possible in that He could make the last, first and the first, last. The implied meaning of this statement was the working of the law of evolution or the law of cause and effect known in the East as *karma* and reincarnation. Today's rich could be tomorrow's poor and today's poor could be tomorrow's rich according to this law. The rich could escape that fate by behaving like the rich farmer in the parable who thought of the worker's welfare more than the convention.

Ruskin's book, written in 1862 had created a great impact in the industrial practices of capitalist economies of the West. Wages were upwardly revised to uphold the ethical value of a living wage. Gandhiji read the book in 1904 while travelling in train from Johannesburg to Durban. "I could not get any sleep that night. I was determined to change my life in accordance with the ideas in the book . . . I later translated the book into Gujarati, entitling it, Sarvodaya, the welfare of all," wrote Gandhiji in his autobiography. Gandhiji had written Sarvodaya in 1908 and in the same year he wrote his famous Hind Swaraj palmphlet inspired by the *sarvodaya* spirit of the book UNTO THIS LAST.

Gandhi introduced the idea of *sarvodaya* to the Indian public when he became involved with India's freedom struggle. He wanted when India became free, India to have a society fired by the ideology of *sarvodaya*. Perhaps, if Gandhiji was not assassinated in 1948, he could have influenced Nehru to mix *sarvodaya* with Nehru's scientific socialism as both of them had the same vision of the overall good of the people at total level of the society.

In a letter written by Gandhiji to Nehru, on November 13, 1945 from Pune, as reproduced in Dorothy Norman's book on Nehru, Gandhiji put on record the mutuality of their vision for India: "Our talk of yesterday made me glad . . . . The impression that I have gathered from our yesterday's talk is that there is not much difference in our outlook. To test this, I put down below the gist of what I have understood. Please correct me if there is any discrepancy.

1.The real question according to you is how to bring about man's highest intellectual, economic, political and moral development. I agree entirely. 2. In this, there should be an equal right and opportunity for all. 3. In other words, there should be equality between the town-dwellers and the villagers in the standard of food and drink, clothing and other living conditions. In order to achieve this equality today, people should be able to produce for themselves the necessaries of life i.e. clothing, foodstuffs, dwellings and lighting and water. 4. Man is not born to live in isolation but is essentially a social animal independent and interdependent. No one can or should ride on another's back. If we try to work out the necessary conditions for such a life, we are forced to the conclusion that the unit of society should be a village or call it a small and manageable group of people who would, in the ideal, be self-sufficient in the matter of their vital requirements as a unit and bound together in bonds of mutual cooperation and inter-dependence."

We are in a situation now, when our idea of being Indians is all blurred: we are not following Nehru's scientific socialism nor Gandhiji's *sarvodaya,* nor are we living the ideals of our epics. What are we following and what do we want? We are not following anything. We have no clear thought pattern as to what we want as a society. The rich among us wallow in their pleasure seeking pursuits while the poor who are the vast majority, aspire for a life that could provide at least the minimum animal comfort at their individual inner being. Come, my dear friends and fellow citizens, let us clear our vision of ourselves as individuals and then as Indians. Let us, using that cleared visions of our being Indians, design the India we dream of. The twelve commissions of the *sarvodaya* model of good governance that follow will help us creating our visions about ourselves as individuals and as Indians.

1. *The Missions of the Republic in the Constitution of India and the State. (The Constitution Missions Commission)*

    This first Commission in the *sarvodaya* good governance model is entrusted with the task of educating every Indian citizen about the missions of the Indian Republic given in the Preamble to the Constitution of India. The missions, the three commitments or resolves of the people of India, as appearing in the Preamble, are treated by this commission as the parameters for designing and managing the social and natural earth systems for the successful evolution of individual citizens at total level of the Indian society.

2. *Advaita and its Cosmogonical and Ontological Relations to the State (Ontology and State Commission)*

    This Commission holds the responsibility of devising ways and means to educate at individual and state levels the interrelationship existing between the evolution of individuals and the evolution of the Universe. This Commission also holds the responsibility of monitoring the contribution of government and civil society institutions in aiding the evolution of citizens at individual and collective levels. This Commission proves to the people in the Republic that the function of state as an institution is to manage the evolution of the people towards their happy and successful living.

3. *The Family Management and its Role as an Aid to the Evolution of the citizens (Family and State Commission)*

Family is the most important of man-made institutions that contribute to the evolution of human beings at individual as well as collective level. This Commission strives to account for the total number of families ward wise, state wise and nation wise and ensures each family gets legitimate development support from all other institutions of the government and civil society.

4. *Education Management and Institutions are Key Aids to the Evolution of individuals and groups (Education and State Commission)*

This Commission is vested with the power to ensure that every individual in the Republic receives adequate level of education both at individual and family levels. Education management and educational institutions are viewed as aids to the successful evolution of people at individual and collective levels.

5. *Health Management and health institutions are Aids to Evolution of People (Health and State Commission*

This Commission is vested with the responsibility of reorganizing country's health institution in such a way that not only the physical aspects of the health needs are taken care of, but also the mental, spiritual and the social aspects of health needs are attended to. After all, health is wealth! And wealth production and its equitable distribution is possible only if the society is of sound spiritual or social health.

6. *Business is the total interdependent commercial activities of a society to sustain and support its successful evolution at individual and collective levels. (Business and State Commission)*

This Commission looks after the total interdependent commercial activities and monitor their constructive and destructive roles to promote a healthy, prosperous and peaceful society after weeding out the negative and destructive activities and their influences on the individuals and society as a whole. Family is the focal point for deciding the good and bad influences of all economic activities. Wealth creation includes education, health, and happy family life apart from other assets.

7. *Ecology Management is a Crucial Area of Good Governance in Times to Come.(Ecology Management and State Commission)*

Ecology, economy and ecumenism are all words emanated from the Greek word, *oikomene* which means the entire earth as a family and they support each other in their mundane expressions of human activities. Managing the interfaces of economy and family with Mother Earth is not only managing pollutions and toxicities in air, water and earth but also includes managing the pollutions and toxicities of our social, economic, cultural spaces at individual and collective mental levels. This Commission manages the natural and cultural ecology for the effective management of personal and societal evolution.

8. *Infrastructure Management is a Major Aid to the Successful Evolution of People Towards Their Happy Living (Infrastructure and State Commission)*

This Commission is responsible for the development, management and optimal utilization of the infrastructural wealth of the nation including the land, forest, mineral and ocean wealth. The citizens have a common rights over these wealth. Every citizen born in the Republic has a right to own a house/land for his or her family. Basic infrastructure to sustain human life and its successful evolution requires, houses, nursing homes and hospitals, schools and colleges, manufacturing and marketing facilities and their interconnecting conveyance facilities, sports and entertainment facilities, agricultural fields and water bodies and food processing facilities. This Commission coordinates with the other Commissions to ascertain their infrastructural needs and timely executions of projects.

9. *Religions and Their Institutions are Essentially Social Systems for Human Evolution Management (Religion and State Commission)*

In a secular society, religions are essentially institutions for managing the evolution of their members towards their successful and happy living. This Commission looks after the interfaces of all religions in the Indian Republic and ensures their cooperative contribution to the well being of the Republic, especially in tune with the Constitutional mandate to promote FRATERNITY among the citizens, assuring their individual dignity and the integrity of the nation.

10. *Relief and Rehabilitation Problems and Timely Solutions are the Duty of the State and Form Part of its Efforts as Aids to Human Evolution (Relief and Rehabilitation & State Commission)*

As human beings, we have the will and imagination to charter our path of evolution towards peaceful and successful life on earth. But, in spite of our innate and acquired skills to protect our lives, we do meet with accidents, unexpected natural and man made disasters. There must be suitable relief giving and rehabilitation systems and practices at total national system level. This Commission is responsible for such rehabilitation systems including orphanages and homes for the elderly people in every neighborhood.

11. *Communication and Mass Media Function in a Democratic Republic is Utmost Crucial for Effective Participation by the People in Implementing the National Goals Adopted in the Constitution. (Mass Media and State Commission)*

India, after emerging as a sovereign democratic republic from the hands of the feudal and fascist administration of the colonial British rulers, had not made any sincere efforts to communicate the Mission Statements in the Preamble to the Constitution of India, to the people at total level of the nation. This was mainly because, the feudal and fascist legacy of the administration inherited by the Indian Republic, did not and could not identify itself with the egalitarian welfare doctrine enshrined in the preamble to the Constitution of India. This Commission will change that deficit and will reenergize the key institutions of the government and the civil society with the spirit of the Preamble, the introductory part of the Constitution of India.

12. ***Governments at Local, State and Central Levels are Only Coordinating Institutions to Steer the Institutions and the People on the Path Shown in the Constitution of India, Especially the Preamble. (Government and State Commission)***

The governance culture inherited from the feudal and fascist British colonial administration by the Indian Republic is highly centric and oppressive and to give justice to the objectives of the Indian Republic as given in the Constitution, this Commission is engaged in designing the decentralized and grass root level governance at total population level.

SUMMING UP

The idea of being Indians is living the life to our maximum divine potential as per the grand scheme of personal and national development contained in the Preamble to the Constitution of India. The grand scheme, inspired by the *advaita* doctrine of the Upanishads which were re-told by Sri Sankaracharya, enables us to develop our physical, mental and spiritual personalities for enjoying the worldly comforts and at the same time climbing the ladder of evolution in the spirit of oneness with our fellowmen and women. Our National Anthem, National Flag and National Emblem are reminders of our divine potential to lead successful personal and community lives.

The Constitutional requirement from each citizen to constitute India into a sovereign, socialist, secular, democratic republic; to secure justice, liberty and equality; and to promote fraternity among citizens, went unheeded by most of us till now. These three supreme actions were expected to create the ideal state of existence for all of us which was the aspiration of our previous generations. Such an aspiration was justified in the eternal verity that the Creator and the created are one and because of this verity, all men and women are born equal and they have the unalienable rights given by their Creator to live and evolve to their maximum potential in autonomous sovereignty and happiness. Democracy and republicanism are premised on this eternal verity.

While the idea of being Indians presented in the Preamble to the Constitution of India is living the life to our maximum divine potential in oneness with our fellow men and women as a common goal, the conditions created by the ruling hierarchies in India was not feasible for such a life for majority of people among us. The reasons as stated repeatedly in this book, were strategic errors made by us by retaining the administrative systems of the colonial British India, for managing the affairs of the Republic of India.

In order to live our life to our maximum divine potential of health, prosperity and peace, we have to replace the feudal, fascist governance systems inherited from the British with democratic and republican administrative systems. A model named as *sarvodya model of good governance* has been presented in this book for the scrutiny and appraisal by my readers and fellow citizens of this great Republic. The model has twelve commissions which together would take care of the need of a democratic republican society and its governments at local, state and central levels.

These twelve commissions will induce us for creating the necessary social structures for replacing the existing British made fascist governance systems. The next chapter, The Making of India, will give a detailed thesis on the application of the *sarvodaya* model and the republican structures of good governance induced by the *sarvodaya* model.

The *sarvodaya model of good governance* is capable of universal application. Since it is an evolutionary model, it will find wider applicability in times to come as more evolved minds will be there on the world stage who will need and accept nothing less.

Chapter Four

The Making of India

When Jawaharlal Nehru went in search of India, through the ancient and recent history (of his lifetime), he discovered that the India, which was Mother India to many, was actually the people who lived in the geographical and cultural spaces known as India over many millennia. The book, Discovery of India, written by him in 1945, was thus about the hopes, agonies, and accomplishments of Indians through the centuries since millennia before Christ. Though Nehru had surmised that Indians consisted of Dravidians who originally lived here and Aryans who were later settlers from elsewhere, Indo-Tibetan monastic literature quoted by Madam Blavatsky and Max Heindel in their writings, suggest that the Dravidians were people who came from the region of Gobi where a flourishing civilization was built by people who came from the sinking Atlantis some 80,000 to 100,000 years ago.

People who came to Gobi from Atlantis were the Semites, the most evolved than the other six races lived in Atlantis. The other races were: Rmoahals, Tlavatlis, Toltecs, Original Turanians, Akadians and Mongolians. It seems, the Cosmic plan was to save the Semites for seeding the future seven Aryan races of the world. For, as the remaining parts of the world became habitable, these Semites moved over to various places including India and were known as the Aryans of India, Babylonian-Assyrian-Chaldean, Persian-Greco-Latin, Celtic and Teutonic-Anglo-Saxon races.

The sixth Aryan race will be seeded by the Russians and Slavs. The seventh Aryan race will come out of the Slavic sixth race. In the meantime, souls of the other races perished in the Atalantian cataclysm, have reborn and multiplied in all the regions where the Semites from Gobi region went to live, according to the monastic records in both East and West.

When the continent Atlantis went under water completely about 12,000 years ago, another set of evolved Semites escaped to India, Egypt and Mexico. The Indian, Egyptian and Mexican(Mayan) civilizations are fundamentally identical in their spiritual concepts and metaphysical teachings conveyed through symbolic stories in the form of myths.

Basically, all these three civilizations have sun and moon deities as focus of worship and ritual as well as magical practices. According to Spencer Lewis, the renowned Rosicrucian, the language spoken by Atlantians at the time of the 2nd batch's exodus from Atlantis, was a language akin to the mixture of Sanskrit and the Persian language used in Zend Avestha. The basic religious symbol, AUM used for the primordial creative energy is also common to Indian,

Egyptian and Mayan civilizations according to Max Toth, author of Pyramid Prophecy.

Today's Indians are thus, the mixture of Aryans coming from Atlantis on both the occasions and those reincarnated from the other negatively evolving races of Atlantis. Such negative evolution and their influences had destroyed the Egyptian, Mayan, Babylonian-Assyrian-Chaldean, and other civilizations. What came to the help of Indians were the personal efforts of many advanced souls known as Rishis, Rama, Sri Krishna, Buddha, Mahavira and Sri Sankaracharya. Because of the management of Evolutionary Law of Karma by the Aryans of India more effectively than the others abroad, through the ways shown by these evolved souls, Indians were able to survive the destructions that had befallen the other civilizations.

Though, Egyptians and Mayans also had equal if not more Cosmic wisdom at their disposal such as, astronomy, architecture, herbal therapy, mathematics, geometry, economics etc, like the Indians, what they did not have enough was the humility and modesty to practice prudent management of Karma or the Evolutionary Law of cause and effect. Fundamental to the effective management of Karma the Law of Evolution was the practice of oneness of humanity based on *advaita* doctrine. The Rama Rajya model for governance and the Bhagavad Gita were the two instruments which helped Indians to stay on course of evolutionary path.

Pythagoras had come all the way from Greece to India to learn the Karma management technique and what Socrates and Plato and Aristotle gave to the world in their teachings in the form of democratic practice on the part of individuals and governments were intended to manage the evolution of people and avoid adverse effect of Karma the Law of Evolution. From what Nehru wrote in the Discovery of India, we can have an idea of the type of life Indians had, till the British came to India: "In 1830, Sir Charles Metcalfe, one of the ablest of British officials in India, described these communities in words which have often been quoted: 'The village communities are little republics having nearly everything they want within themselves; and almost independent of foreign relations. They seem to last where nothing else lasts. This union of the village communities, each one forming a separate little state in itself . . . is in a high degree conducive to their happiness, and to the enjoyment of a great portion of freedom and independence."

Even American and French societies after their revolutions to establish themselves as republican societies in the 1780s, could not match the republican life Indians had till the British East India Company and British government ravaged India. American and French revolutions were led by people who were influenced by eternal verities taught by the esoteric schools affiliated to the Egyptian mystic traditions. In the post-revolution society, in France and the United States of America, a reasonable level of universal brotherhood and corresponding elevation of standard of living for common people, have been instituted and for this, the credit should go to the Egyptian spiritual tradition which influenced the teachings of Moses and Jesus, both of whom taught the oneness among the human race and the Creator and the consequent oneness or brotherhood existed among the people themselves.

But unfortunately, after the Indian revolution and subsequent attainment of freedom from British tyranny, the

Indian society has not been able to taste the oneness and brotherhood promised by the leaders of the revolution. Only 20% of the people of India has a decent standard of living while another 20% has a modicum of good standard of living and the bulk i.e. 60% has a poor or very poor standard of living. Pioneered by Mahatma Gandhi and supported by a horde of mystics and followers of *vedanta dharma* and *advaita* doctrine, Indian independence revolution ought to have brought about a universal brotherhood and consequent elevation of standard of living for the common people of India.

We must remember that before the British came to India, we had village republics here and people were generally happy and peaceful. Though, we had Mughal rulers from outside coming here and ruling us for over a thousand years, they had integrated themselves into the Indian life style and became Indians, as Nehru wrote in the Discovery of India. The custodians of Hindu sacred and secret teachings were diligent enough to have kept the vast wealth of these texts away from the Mughals so that they could not be subjected to forced alteration or amendments according to Islamic doctrines. Madam Blavatsky had testified to this fact in her voluminous writings on Hinduism.

We must also remember that Indians possessed the most advanced knowledge in astronomy, mathematics, therapeutics, agricultural sciences, environmental sciences, architecture, carpentry, handicrafts and horde of useful skills, including spiritual interpersonal skills necessary for making daily living a pleasant experience for the community during and from the Vedic period. Francois M. Voltaire(1694-1774) had recorded in his writings that Pythagoras, the great philosopher mystic had visited India and acquainted himself with the advanced geometric principles from Hindu scholars of Vedic mathematical sciences. Moreover, great physicists such as Pierre Simon de Laplace(1749-1827), Julius R. Oppenheimer(1904-1967), Albert Einstein(1879-1955), John Archibald Wheeler (1911-2008),Werner Heisenberg(1901-76), Erwin Schrodinger(1887-1961), Dr. Carl Sagan(1934-1996), Dr. Lin Yutang (1895-1976), and mathematician Alfred North Whitehead(1861-1947) and the French writer Romaine Rolland(1866-1944) are some of the famous personalities who have had expressed in their lifetime that modern science has come closer to the Vedic sciences.

According to economic historian Angus Madison, India was the leading economic power in the world till 1000AD and during the Mughal rule India's GDP was 27% of the world's total in 1700AD. But when the British rulers left India, its GDP was a mere 3% in 1950. In 2013 this figure is still below the 3% mark and in fact this is the highest level achieved during the last 63 years after we became a republic. But why are we not able to take off and soar in the sky of prosperity? The answer has been given in earlier chapters, in fact repetitively, and which is that our Republic is administered with the feudal-fascist governance apparatus used by the British to subjugate, suppress, loot and empty the coffers of India for nearly 200 years since 1757. But there is more than mere being administered with British governance agencies:

There is a gem of a thought introduced by Jawaharlal Nehru in his book, *The Discovery of India*. He says, there are two sections of civilization living side by side in any country, one, evolved, more democratic and civilized while the other less evolved, feudal, brutal and uncivilized. In case of England also this theory of Nehru was valid. "Which of these two Englands came to India? The England of Shakespeare and Milton, of noble speech and writing and brave deed, of political revolution and the struggle for freedom, of science and technical progress, or the England of the savage penal code and brutal behavior, of entrenched feudalism and reaction? For there were two Englands, just as in every country there are these two aspects of national character and civilization.

The two Englands live side by side, influencing each other, and cannot be separated; nor could one of them come to India forgetting completely the other. Yet in every major action one plays the leading role, dominating the other, *and it was inevitable that the wrong England should play that role in India and should come in contact with and encourage the wrong India in the process* . . . The British who came to India were not political or social revolutionaries; they were conservatives representing the most reactionary social class in England, and England was in some ways one of the most conservative countries in Europe."

I am taking Nehru's statements made in the book, *Discovery of India,* as quoted above, as the most significant insight provided to his followers and fellow citizens of India for rebuilding their nation as soon as it was freed from the cruel clutches of the British rulers. Sixty six years after that crucial and momentous event, India's freedom from the British brutalities of nearly two centuries, having seen that Nehru's insight went unnoticed and unutilized, I have the fortune of bringing this insight of Nehru for you my dear readers and fellow citizens of this great country.

As we have seen that India is actually the people living in its geographical and cultural space, the quality of Indians will decide the quality of India—the geographical and cultural space (socio-economic institutions) of India. Therefore our idea of being Indians will determine what kind of India we are going to make. You will remember, just few paragraphs back, we had raised a question to ourselves: why post-Independence India failed to bring India back to the pre-British stage of village independence and prosperity? By now, you might have got the clue for an answer to that question: The crude feudal England who ruled India had gone back but the crude feudal India had taken over charge along with the ruling apparatus created by the feudal England specially to manage the real estate that was India.

Of course, the clue was taken from Nehru's insight that every nation has two sections of people existing side by side, the one self-seeking, feudal minded and the other democratic and egalitarian minded or talking in terms of civilizational direction, the one positively evolving and the other negatively evolving. Nehru wrote:

"Feudal land lords who came to India to rule over India from England had the landlord's view of the world. To them India was a vast estate belonging to the East India Company, and the landlord was the best and the natural representative of his estate and his tenants. That view continued even after the East India Company handed over its estate of India to the British Crown, being paid very handsome compensation at India's cost. (Thus began the public debt of India. It was India's purchase money, paid by India.) The British Government of India then became the landlords (or landlords' agents). For all practical purposes, they considered themselves 'India', just as the Duke of Devonshire might be considered 'Devonshire' by his peers. The millions of people who lived and functioned in India were just some kind of landlord's tenants who had to pay their rents and taxes and to keep their place in the natural feudal order." Don't you think, we have with us at present a similar sort of dispensation existing with India's middle class that snatched all economic benefits of governance during the past 66 years, treating the entire land as its Dukedom.

"Though books and old monuments and past cultural achievements helped to produce some understanding of India, they did not satisfy me or give me the answer I was looking for. Nor could they, for they dealt with a past age, and I wanted to know if there was any real connection between that past and the present. The present for me, and for many others like me, was an odd mixture of medievalism, appalling poverty and misery and a somewhat superficial modernism of the middle classes. I was not an admirer of my own class or kind, and yet inevitably I looked to it for leadership in the struggle for India's salvation; *that middle class felt caged and circumscribed and wanted to grow and develop itself. Unable to do so within the framework of British rule, a spirit of revolt grew against this rule, and yet this spirit was not directed against the structure that crushed us. It sought to retain it and control it by displacing the British. These middle classes were too much the product of that structure to challenge it and seek to uproot it."* These words of Nehru were not only true about India's middle class in the British India but true also about the middle class in post-Independence India till now and may be so for a long time to come, unless a mass movement sweeps across the nation sooner than later. (Italics by the author for emphasis)

The structure Nehru talked about, had prevented even Nehru, in his 17 years as the Prime Minister of India, from changing the impoverished feudal British India into a prosperous republican India in spite of the fact that it was he who moved the resolution containing republican India's objectives in the Constituent Assembly of India in 1946 which ultimately became the missions of the Republic of India as stated in the Preamble to the Constitution of India. The Mission Statements of the Indian Republic given in the Preamble to the Constitution of India were the guide lines for changing the 'structure that crushed us.'

So, my dear readers and fellow citizens of India, a great nation, that is healthy, prosperous, peaceful and happy as we had dreamt about India, could not be realized because of the continuance of the 'structure that crushed us.' The onus is on us now to change that structure. Since the making of a healthy, prosperous and peaceful India is primarily the making of Indians healthy, prosperous and peaceful, let us explore how the *sarvodaya model of good governance* could be applied for making all of us Indians happy and successful in our lives.

APPLYING *SARVODAYA MODEL OF GOOD GOVERNANCE* FOR PERSONAL AND NATIONAL DEVELOPMENT

1. *Constitution Missions Commission*

Perhaps, very few citizens have thought about the roles the Mission Statements of our Republic, as given in the Preamble to the Constitution of India, could play in the making of India which is in our dreams and which was in the dreams of many generations of Indians. Since India is Indians, the roles played by these Mission Statements for the development—the physical, mental and spiritual growth—of all of us, the citizens of India, assume great importance. It was on the basis of these missions of the Indian Republic listed in the Preamble, that the future of Indians, liberated from the worst kind of colonial subjugation by England for over two hundred years, was to be designed for a healthy, prosperous, happy and peaceful living at total level of the Indian society on a continuous and permanent basis.

The Constitution Missions Commission recognized what Nehru said about the middle class of India and accordingly takes note of the fact that due to its act of retaining the 'structure that crushed us' for running the Republic, not only that the Mission Statements of the Republic could not be translated into experiential comforts for the people of this country, but the 'crushing' of people had also not abated and is still going on in our republican India! For realizing the Mission Statements of the Indian Republic as contained in the Preamble to the Constitution of India, we need to take various urgent steps. Some urgent steps needed are given here for your intellectual appreciation and putting into action if appropriate:

1. *Let us recognize and debate at national level the Nehruvian analysis that the England which came to rule India was of the savage penal code and brutal behavior, of entrenched feudalism and reaction or the wrong England as Nehru called it and this wrong England joined hands with the wrong India of entrenched feudalism and reaction for ruling India.*

2. *Let us recognize and debate at national level that the Indian middle class who fought for India's freedom wanted only the British to go from India and not their systems of governance even though they were crushing Indians, as Nehru had rightly commented so in his book, Discovery of India.*

3. *Let us also recognize and debate the fact that the Constitution of India was written by Members of the Constituent Assembly who were true representatives of the Indian middle class that was the product of the wrong England and the wrong India of the savage penal code and brutal behavior, entrenched feudalism and reactionary conservatism, as Nehru had rightly described in Discovery of India.*

4. *The Constitution of India as it stands today, is a representation of progressive and conservative ideas. While its Preamble represents the most noble and progressive ideas that could steer the Indian Republic on the road of right evolution towards successful living for the people at 100% level, the texts comprising various Articles do not reflect the republican character of the Preamble satisfactorily. Since the Preamble was to serve as the objectives of the Republic to be achieved, the details worked out in the rest of the Constitution had not given justice to the objectives in the Preamble as they tended to sub-serve the interests of the feudal middle class. The Constitutional direction of many Articles was to continue the revenue model of the British feudal government.*

A remedy for this anomaly is to add many more fundamental rights for home, food, income, health, education, peace etc. to make the right to life given in the Constitution really meaningful and useful.

Right to life in feudal society and a republican society differs like night and day. A feudal society will not feel the pangs in the life lived by a slave and a poor man, a hungry and the under-fed and a prisoner who is a poor man, while a republican society will and should!

5. *The Preamble to the Constitution of India must be treated as the Mission Statements of the Indian Republic and as such it should be brought to the notice of the citizens of India in all walks of life. All homes and schools should be targeted.*

6. *Once the necessary amendments to the Constitutional provisions have been made to include rights to food, house/land, education at university level, health delivery at home, income security and social harmony, the book of Indian Constitution should be made a compulsory reading material available at all homes like scriptures of religion*

7. *All political parties must incorporate the Mission Statements of Indian Republic as contained in the Preamble to the Constitution of India as main compulsory parts of their objectives and Election Commission of India should supervise adherence of this step by the political parties.*

8. *Members of all political parties must be made duty bound to serve the people of the Republic of India as per the spirit of the Mission Statements in the Preamble to the Constitution. When they join a political party, their sole purpose must be to serve the people of India voluntarily and their sustenance question should arise*

only when they are full time into public service. Their service should not be restricted to fund collection and party development. Their real duty is always towards their brothers and sisters, the Indian fellowmen and women.

Every party member should have the objective of community development as the beginning of their career and for this he or she would start working in the local neighborhood community taking up development programs in education, health, housing, income generation, cleanliness, and environment fields.

2. *Ontology and the State Commission*

Ontology, according to the dictionary meaning, is the study of being in terms of both the seen and unseen realms of existence. At deeper level, the study delves into the nature of human being and the nature of Universe, and then the relation between the nature of human being, its growth at physical, mental and spiritual levels and the nature of Universe, its origin, its process of becoming the various units of the un-manifested and manifested worlds.

In a good governance model, the place for ontology is exalted indeed. At the early stage of civilization, religions of the ancient times were capable of taking care of the ontological need of governance at personal and community levels. With the introduction of anthropomorphic teachings of religions, ontological teachings have retreated from open forums to esoteric brotherhoods.

A scrutiny of the history of political thinking reveals that social philosophers who had either glimpses of ontological teachings of esoteric brotherhoods or were of evolved minds capable of intuitively sensing ontological truths were the main thrust behind the movement of establishing democratic and republican governments across the world from the medieval period. The ontological truth of *advaita* that the Creator had become the created men and women through the process of evolution and therefore all men and women possess equal rights to live and evolve autonomously towards fulfilling their life's missions of happiness and peace, was the premise on which all democratic and republican thinking have been constructed.

As citizens of India, whether women or men, you and I are sovereign individuals with destiny of autonomous evolution towards our life's mission of attaining happiness and peace. We have made commitments to ourselves that we will honor this sovereignty of autonomous evolution at both personal and total population level when we constituted India into a republic. But, it appears that both at personal and state level, we have forgotten this commitment. The 'sovereign, secular, socialist and democratic' aspects of the republic have not been given the importance they deserve.

Or else, India would not be holding the world's worst record in Global Hunger Index-2012, at 22.9. Among 79 countries surveyed by the International Food Policy Research Institute, India, ranked 65th and with a GHI of 22.9, is in a highly deplorable position, as a score above 10 is indicative of hunger and starvation at wider level in a society. The GHI is constructed with indices of the proportions of undernourished people, underweight children and child mortality in a given society or a country. China has a GHI of 5 in the 2012 GHI report.

After Independence, India has made 200% progress in per capita income. In 1947, India's per capita income was $50 per annum which in 2012 stood at an average of $1000 per annum. But, the hunger index had not made proportionate improvement. In 1990, India's GHI score as monitored by IFPRI was 30.3, which fell to 22.6 in 1996. But again rose to 24.2 in 2001 and stood at 22.9 in 2012, much closer to 1996 levels. What this dissonance in income growth and hunger persistence indicates is that the economic development made by India was restricted to the middle class India, which according to Nehru, was the product of the feudal-fascist policies of the colonial British government.

Ontology and State Commission has the responsibility of changing the feudal mindset of the ruling middle class of India into democratic republican mindset. The feudal mind is self seeking and self aggrandizing while the democratic and republican mind is egalitarian and altruistic. Elsewhere in this book, we have seen how appreciative was Dr. Man Mohan Singh, India's current Prime Minister of the feudal British system of government, inherited by the Indian Republic, at a lecture session he had at Oxford University not many years ago! It was an admission on his part that India is still under a feudal minded ruling hierarchy. Even otherwise, during India's journey through all these years since Nehru wrote in his book, *Discovery of India* in 1945 that the middle class in India wanted only to displace the British and not their systems which crushed us, no political, no philosophical, no doctrinal discourse arose from any section of Indian society on the anomaly of Indian democratic republic continuing with the feudal British systems of governance. This again is the vital clue that the ruling middle class of India is out and out feudal and fascist.

Our attempt to change the feudal governance structure into republican democratic one, will succeed only when the required attitudinal change of Indians has been wrought by ontological perspectives such as:

1. *The evolution of human beings and the evolution of the Universe are inter-related as humans are integral parts of the Universe.*

2. *Since the causeless Cause or the First Cause is the Supreme Source of all seen and unseen parts of the Universe, it is only logical to think that the First Cause has become the Universe, including the humans. All leading religions at their core, dwell on this eternal verity and try to remind us so.*

3. *Ontological perceptions such as 'aham brahmasmi' and 'tat tvam asi' ('I am brahman' and 'you are that') have prompted evolved minds among humans to design systems to aid human evolution on the right track in tune with the evolutionary laws of the Universe.*

4. *Good governance systems such as democratic and republican governments are thus aids to correct human evolution towards attaining the divine perfection or the evolutionary goal of perfection as healthy, prosperous and peaceful persons at individual and total population levels.*

5. *Ontological view holds that the human personality consists of body, mind and spirit which are sub-divided again as:*

> Body: physical body, vital body and desire body
> Mind: mental body
> Spirit: human spirit, life spirit and divine spirit

6. *All political, economic and social actions by governments, other institutions and individual citizens should function as aids to the evolution of citizens as triune beings of body, mind and spirit.*

7. *The Constitutional requirements of constituting India into a sovereign, socialist, secular, democratic republic; securing political, economic and social justice; liberty of thought, expression, belief, faith and worship; equality of status and opportunity; and promoting fraternity among citizens are goals impossible to achieve without imbibing by the citizens, the ontological perspectives of oneness among human beings and oneness between human beings and the Supreme Source of all creations. This oneness provides the status of gods to human beings—who are indeed gods in evolution. The value and validity of democracy hinges on this supreme truth. All scriptures proclaim so too.*

8. *Government as an institution responsible for managing the evolution of citizens towards their successful living, has the onus of making citizens imbibe the ontological perspectives of life and its evolution.*

3. *Family and the State Commission*

In a good governance model, the place occupied by Family is as high as ontology or even greater than the other two Commissions described so far, because, family is the first institution consciously and deliberately designed for managing the evolution of people in the right direction towards obtaining their divine perfection in both temporal and spiritual matters. Family's role in the management of evolution of people for successful living is greatest among all the man-made institutions. Especially the family consisting of parents, children and grand parents where love for each other is natural and genuine. Children born with defects in body or mind or spirit could get love and support only in a family and it is very rare that persons without any defect in any of these three spheres of personality are present in any given society.

Indian society in earlier periods had the four *ashramas* of life known as the *brahmacharya-ashrama,* the *garhastya-ashrama,* the *vanaprastha-ashrama* and the *thapasya-ashrama* which were designs for effective management of human personality in all the three spheres of body, mind and spirit. We may not have such designs in our modern society, but a family could provide the environment for its members for reaping the benefits of the four *ashramas.* There are families in India who provide their members the four *ashrama*-type atmosphere and citizens coming from such families are good assets to the nation. But such families are very few in number indeed in the present-day Indian society.

The *guru-kula* system of education where pupils stay at the teacher's place till they complete their studies and are able to take up the house-hold responsibilities, was the common practice in ancient India. *Guru-kula* is an example of a social system specially designed for managing the evolution of citizens. The teachers in *guru-kula* were trained in astrology and aura reading besides the regular subjects of study. The teachers could see with the help of astrology and auric reading the soul or sub-conscious nature brought forward by the students from their previous births. Depending on the type and depth of negative traits found in the reading, the teacher designs corrective physical and mental exercises as well as the methods of teaching the regular study material to suit the peculiar need of each student.

The Greek mystic philosopher, Pythagoras who had visited India some twenty-six hundred years ago had copied *guru-kula* system in his country. Plato had also employed *guru-kula* method of astrological and auric reading for diagnosing the special needs of his student disciples who attended his academy, according to Bertrand Russell, author of *A History of Western Philosophy.*

In our society, we may not have *guru-kula* system, but what the student misses in the *guru-kula* could be made available in family by the loving parents who would recognize their child's negative traits from the early stages of child's growth and provide necessary corrections. Educated mother and father trained to raise the children towards their evolutionary heights are the keys to the success of a family and such successful families are the keys to a successful nation of responsible citizens.

Basically, India's problems at present are those created by families failing to produce honest, morally upright and socially committed citizens for building a sovereign, socialist, secular, democratic republic. The reason behind this failure is the lack of a national policy to create honest, morally upright and socially committed Indians. The reason for this lack is the structuring the Indian Republic with the feudal-fascist structures of administration, judiciary and police, left behind by the colonial British rulers. The family is the ideal resource or aid for the proper evolution of its members. In the same way, the nation republic is the ideal resource to the families, for the evolution of the people residing in them. And, a nation republic as a resource to its people will succeed only if the families in the republic are able to become proper resources to their members for their evolution towards their successful living.

Rajiv Gandhi had introduced the human resource management concept of the corporate world to the government of India by bringing health, family welfare and education under Human Resource Development Ministry. But, they did not stick together and at present only education is handled by HRD ministry. Viewing people as resources to the nation or to corporates or to the government is the function of a feudal-capitalist world view. For the British colonial government in India, the nation was the government and the people were its vassals. And the governments in the Independent India had inherited this outlook through the inheritance of the legacy of colonial administration.

In a democratic republic, the government and the nation state are the instruments for managing the evolution of people for successful living and this goal is best achieved through the development of families as aids to people's evolution towards successful living. Family and State Commission has the responsibility to convert the Indian Republic as resource to develop families as human development aids or as aids to evolution of people for successful living. Some essential steps towards that goal are:

1. *In the good governance model, family as an aid to successful human evolution, consists of legally wedded*

husband, wife and their children with or without the parents of either the husband, or wife or in special situation, parents of both husband and wife.

2. *With ontological perspectives guiding all the Commissions in our good governance model, gay, lesbian and unwed single parent families are totally unacceptable simply because, the evolutionary dual polarities are missing in such families and are therefore anti-evolutionary.*

3. *It was only in recent times that modern science has got a clue as to how culture could influence evolution, whereas the occult or spiritual sciences known as metaphysics had that information a long, long time ago, reckoned in millennia. On June 16, 2008, Newspapers and electronic media all over the world had reported the scientific finding that the brain area that decides sexual preferences in lesbians and heterosexual men was same and so was the brain area of gay men and heterosexual women. The brain development of lesbians and gay men which orient them towards same sex mating had started right in their mothers' womb, according to the scientist Ivanka Savic, who conducted the study at the Karolinska Institute in Stockholm, Sweden. A practice of same sex cohabitation indulged in adolescence in this life, could end up in permanent same sex preference through reincarnation phenomena over a period covering few life times. It is because of this, all major religions had prohibited same sex practices from ancient times. There is a possibility of a whole race becoming homosexual due to the culture-gene coevolution and then getting destroyed by mother nature, as depicted in the Sodom Gomorrah story. Many Western democratic governments have accepted same sex marriages and open*

same sex cohabitation unaware of the cultural impact such practice could have on genetic transmission through the coming generations and the possibility of becoming homosexual at total level of the society. Such a situation would contradict the evolutionary goals of mother nature and consequently would invite punishment from her in the form of total annihilation and creation of a new race as is her wont for natural selection.

4. *No institution in India, including the government, is engaged in producing honest, morally upright and socially committed citizens for building a sovereign, socialist, secular, democratic republic at present. The reason we have seen, is the lack of a national policy to create honest, morally upright and socially committed Indians. The Family and State Commission responds to this need with deliberate interaction with all major institutions both inside and outside the government.*

5. *How culture can influence gene formation and variation have been reported extensively in science journals dealing with genetics and psychology from early 1980s. As a proof, they say drinking milk by adults was not a habit some ten thousand years ago. But some time later, some communities started raising cattle as part of their economic activities and using milk in various form of food have gradually changed the gene to change itself into a gene that promoted digestion and assimilation of milk. For scientists, this empiric evidence of culture influencing gene and then gene influencing behavior to form culture may be new, but to the sages and seers of olden times, this interrelation between culture and gene was known and they communicated about it to the common folks in ethical stories as major factors of human evolution.*

Family is the most important institution for creating cultural forms because, it can push forward human evolution upward by inculcating positive behavior patterns in children, parents, grand parents and even neighbors, or it can push it backward by negative behavior patterns inculcated by various members. Family and State Commission responds to this most important need by emphasizing on both intrinsic character building and extrinsic community and nation building by families throughout the country at total level of the population.

India's need for building a sovereign, socialist, secular, democratic republic as well as securing justice, liberty and equality and promoting fraternity has to be inculcated at family level first and then at other institution levels. If family fails to do so, then all the efforts put in by other institutions in that direction will be futile.

6. *Family and State Commission is responsible to ensure women's equality, education and economic independence promoted and processed at family level as national culture begins in the form of communication and corresponding behavior in families. Crimes against women such as rape, eve teasing and domestic cruelty by men could be brought to nil if boys in families are taught to treat their sisters and women generally with equal status and respect as they themselves expect for them.*

7. *Can we imagine the well being of Indians without owning homes or land to build homes on? No, obviously!*

Can you imagine the well being of Indians without having enough schools, colleges, nursing homes, hospitals and proper staff to run them? Similarly can you imagine Indians being happy without earning enough income that could give them a comfortable living? The Family and State Commission wants the nation to plan its economic developments with family in the center of focus. At present, India's built up assets in these sectors could cater to only one third of Indians with good standard of living.

8. *If Indians want to make their republic corruption-free, then they have to start from their own families with the first step of practicing honesty, truthfulness, fraternity, justice, liberty and equality for all in their own families. Similarly, if Indians want to be healthy, prosperous and peaceful, first they have to create health, prosperity and peace in the minds of parents. Also, honest tax payers and charitable philanthropists are made in families.*

4. *Education and the State Commission*

The institution of education should be handled by the Government at Central, state and local levels as an aid to the evolution of people who are gods in evolution as per our *Sarvodaya* Good Governance Model. Justice, liberty, equality and fraternity are main objectives of the Constitution of India and educational institutions were supposed to spread awareness about these objectives. But today, education field is replete with the violation of the spirit of these objectives.

We have schools for the poor run by Municipalities; schools for lower middle class run by Government; schools for average middle class run by average private managements;

schools for upper middle class people run by upper middle class managements; schools for upper class run by upper class managements; and lastly we have schools for super rich people run by super rich managements.

In schools run by upper class and super rich families, a major part of the student population comprises those from families of politicians and bureaucrats. The other part comprises business families.

On one side, Governments at Centre and in states struggle to raise reservation quota level in higher education and Government and private jobs, due to the socio-economic imbalances in the Indian society and on the other, Governments at Centre and in states encourage socio-economic imbalances through the education system. Students from these schools invariably end up in their own social strata in their adult life perpetuating the class distinctions.

As an aid to evolution, education must satisfy an individual in two ways. First, it must give him/her necessary inputs to develop his/her inner personality making him/her a respectable and valuable citizen and second, it should make him/her well read and informed to make a living from a suitable career or business.

As a nation of unity and harmony with so many diverse languages, religions and cultural regions, India needs uniform education contents in all her schools from north to south and from east to west.

The Education and State Commission is responsible for monitoring the information contents in the institutional networks of the Indian society so that each institution would become a perfect aid in making every individual born in India a fulsome personality capable of creating health, wealth and social harmony at individual and community level.

At least some programs as listed below should be implemented immediately:

1. *India should take up plans for neighborhood schools and colleges. To fulfill the missions India had undertaken in its Constitution, every village and urban neighborhood should be equipped with all conveniences required for a decent living.*

2. *Right to Education Act should cover compulsory education up to graduation when a person is considered to have mastered enough life skills to steer his or her life towards a known or selected destination in life. At present compulsory education is insisted up to 14 years of age and a student would be in 8th or 9th standard by that age. A poor student would be compelled to discontinue from his studies before completing his high school degree according to the existing RTE Act. It is difficult to understand how the Indian Government which treats education as the human development resource could be content with this piece of enactment.*

3. *As a matter of duty, the Government should make equal opportunities for all citizens to earn life skills by the time they become capable of leading independent responsible lives. Normally a college education or two or three years of technical education after high school*

seem to be proper for earning sufficient skills to conduct oneself in life and contribute to the national economy.

4. *At present, there is very little focus on citizen skills to be included in life skills learning in India. What use is there of a person standing at the summit of success in terms of profession, fame and prosperity, if he or she has not had proper citizenship training for himself or herself or if he or she has not been able to produce useful citizens out of his/her children? Government has the duty to make every home the centre of citizenship training first and then only the educational institution should become venue for such skills.*

5. *India's spending on education and research is one of the lowest among world's nations. Reckoned in terms of GDP, India spends less than 1% on research and 4% on education. These figures should be doubled if we want Indians to be educated at total level of the population and self-reliant and entrepreneurial as a society.*

6. *Mostly, India is still following an education pattern that was followed by British India for creating job force to run and exploit India's natural resources and collect revenue. We have not yet sat together to design an education system which will make every Indian sovereign and autonomous in innate evolution and attain his or her divine heights in health, prosperity and social harmony making India attain its given Constitutional objectives of health, prosperity and peace at 100% population level.*

7. *The institution of education consisting of teachers, managements of schools and colleges, government ministries and departments, the text book publishers, parents and the students together should act united as a major aid to people's evolution towards successful*

living. This view is necessary to upgrade their quality of services.

8. *Education through the mass media consisting of print, electronic and other visual forms of communications needs to be formalized as effective tool for citizenship training and nation building in accordance with the Mission Statements of Constitution of India, as contained in the Preamble to the Constitution of India. Besides, the mass media should campaign for the replacement of the British governance systems which still are virtually continuing the British rule in India blocking the sovereignty i.e. the autonomous evolution of the Indian citizens. Since most of the ownerships of media are controlled by middle class or upper class, communication contents fail to support the issues of 70% of the Indian population falling below the middle class status and impatiently waiting to rise from its perennial poverty to the pristine glory it used to enjoy among world's nations before the arrival of the 'wrong section' of the British to do business first and then to subdue and exploit us. We want an education system which will train and equip people to replace the British systems of governance retained by our founding fathers, inadvertently.*

5. *Health and the State Commission*

All of us are familiar with the old adage that health is wealth. Now, what exactly is health? Is it mere absence of disease? Is full fledged health care service covering the total population, able to keep disease away from people? When we ponder over the idea of being Indians and the making of India, is only physical health valid for our consideration? Answers to these questions will enable us to grasp the full dimension of the concept of health that contributes to holistic personality of a citizen and the national synergy produced by such citizens.

First of all, the adage is quite true because, without health, all wealth accumulated will be useless, as in sickness of body or mind or spirit, we seldom are able to enjoy life and its various hues of comforts. If we are sick, no amount of wealth can make us happy. On the other hand if we do not have wealth but are blessed with health, at least we have the hope that we can make wealth as we go ahead in life. Secondly, health is that state in which we are free from sickness of body, mind and spirit and negative social conditions and are in full functional efficiency enabling us to evolve successfully and lead successful lives.

Health care services provided at total level of the population may be able to cure diseases as and when they occur, but fail to keep the population healthy on a permanent basis because, our society is never free from disease making causes such as germs, pollution of air and water, diet imbalances, malnutrition and psycho-socio-economic turmoil. Talking of psycho-socio-economic turmoil, Indian society was never free from such adverse conditions not only during the British rule but even after the people's rule in the independent India! The frightening reality before us is that our society had sealed its health forever when it embraced the colonial British India's governance structure.

The health of a nation is made not only by the health care services available to the citizens, but also by the mental, social and spiritual conditions prevailing in its family and community life. The administrative, police, judicial and political structure in our country, inherited from the feudal-fascist colonial British government, are conducive to the production of a sick society out of us.

"India has the dubious distinction of being home to the world's largest number of sick people. It is also home to the largest number of malnourished people. Dig a bit deeper and you will find a bizarre contradiction: we seem to have got the worst of both poor and rich countries. About 37% of deaths are caused by infectious diseases such as TB, malaria, diarrhea, etc while 53% are due to metabolic or non-communicable diseases such as heart ailments and diabetes," says a social impact report featured by Times of India on October 25, 2012.

In India one maternal death is being reported every 10 minutes. India recorded around 57,000 maternal deaths in 2010, which translate into a whopping six every hour and one every 10 minutes, according to a UN report released in July 2012. "With almost 19,000 children under five years of age dying every day across the world, India tops the list of countries with the highest number of 16.55 lakh such deaths in 2011, according to a UN agency. The 'Child Mortality Estimates Report 2012' released by UNICEF in New York has said that in 2011, around 50 per cent of global under-five deaths occurred in just five countries of India, Nigeria, the Democratic Republic of the Congo, Pakistan and China. Incidentally, India's toll is higher than the deaths in Nigeria, Democratic Republic of Congo and Pakistan put together. While there have been 7.56 lakh deaths in Nigeria during the last year, Democratic Republic of the Congo accounts for 4.65 lakh deaths and Pakistan 3.52 lakh deaths of under-five children during 2011," reported NDTV on September, 13, 2012.

When we are venturing to make the India of our dream on the basis of the Mission Statements contained in the Preamble to the Constitution of India and derive the idea of being Indians from the accomplishments of those missions, the state of India's health as a nation is crucial indeed. The administrative, judicial and police systems we inherited from the colonial British government have contributed to the health problems of India in two ways. One, the stress and strain inflicted to the society by the administrative staff with bribery and harrowing delays in service delivery; by the courts with inordinate delay of justice disbursement to the tune of twenty to thirty years in cases numbering more than 35 million; and by the police with atrocious violation of personal sovereignty of people in arresting and detaining for days, months and years without assigning any valid reasons. Two, the dysfunction of health system-network in the country caused by the entrenched feudal and fascist mindset of the government personnel, including the ministers and their political supporters.

The Health and the State Commission is vested with the responsibility of reorganizing country's health structure in such a way that not only the physical aspects of the health needs are taken care of, but also the mental, spiritual and the social aspects of health needs are attended to. Key programs envisaged are:

1. *The health institution in the country must be treated as a key aid to the successful evolution of people towards their successful living. The health planners, doctors in the ministries of Central and State Governments, doctors, nurses, paramedical staff and the hospital and nursing home managements are treated as resources for*

the successful evolution of people of the Indian Republic of which they are partakers.

2. *Neighborhood hospitals of primary, secondary and tertiary levels should be established in all Panchayat and Municipality Wards in all states of India.*

3. *All medical facilities in all these 3 levels of hospitals or nursing homes should be made available uniformly to all sections of the society irrespective of their social and economic class, gender or age.*

4. *All medical services in all these facilities should be made affordable to all sections of society through insurance schemes made compulsorily binding on all through participation from government, employers, people's cooperatives, and the insured members.*

5. *Since allopathic medicines are mostly agents of unanticipated side effects of toxic nature and are capable of removing only the symptoms and not the root causes of diseases, more emphasis should be given to Indian traditional Ayurveda medicine for wider use by people of all economic and social classes across the country.*

6. *Right to health is not legislated as yet but, the right to life assured as a fundamental right in the Constitution of India should implicitly hold out the promise of right to health without which life is not possible for a citizen as health is defined as the functional soundness of a person at physical, mental, spiritual and social levels. If you cannot express yourself physically, mentally, spiritually and socially, your life is not useful to you or anybody and thus meaningless. Government of India must make healthcare policy not only for preventing and curing diseases but also for building holistic health—physical, mental, spiritual and social health— of citizens and make health care delivery on 24x7x365*

basis to every family in the country irrespective of social and economic class barriers.

7. In per capita expenditure on health care including both preventive and curative measures, India is at 141st position among 156 nations with spending figure of $124 per annum including both government and private spending. First position is occupied by USA with a health spend of $7960. China at 108th position spends $347. As a share of GDP, India's spend is 4.2% out of which Government spends only around 1% and the remainder is spent by private sector. During 2012-2017 period, Government's share will rise to 2.5%. Unless the Government and the private sector increase their share by three-fold with immediate effect, the 70% of population who is left out of the prosperity planning of the country, will remain malnourished and anaemic for the rest of their lives. Without such an increase in health spending, the picture is not going to be encouraging for us to cherish a pleasant idea of being Indians nor the idea of making the India of our dream.

8. Malnutrition and anaemia affect almost 70% of the population of India. The arithmetic is simple. The growing middle class accounts for 20 to 30% and people in that class have enough to eat and drink. But the rest of the population making the 70% is that category which includes those who now famously are described as earning less than Rs.26 a day and those who earn the national minimum wage of Rs.100 a day. The official version of undernourished population of children and women are available but about men both UN and national governments are silent nor are men subjected to any malnutrition survey!

Officially, 50% of women and 42% of children are malnourished and anaemic in India. Men are not any better, because they abuse their body with habits of drinking and chewing tobacco based products, thus wasting whatever advantage they had over their women in terms of earning and freedom of choosing good food.

Unless India raises the opportunity of people in the 70% category with immediate effect by raising the minimum wages 12000-15,000 per month, and increase thereby the purchasing power of individuals and families, malnutrition will continue for long, long time in India. But as long as the feudal fascist attitude of the middle class, steered by the ruling hierarchy in the country does not change to democratic and republican, raising the minimum wages and the value of labour of poor will remain a non-starter in India.

Kerala's example is worth following by workers of other Indian states. The daily wage of workers is 450-550 and skilled laborers in certain trades even get upward Rs.500 to Rs.1000 in Kerala and workers from Northern states are finding it beneficial to visit Kerala and enter its labour market. This unusual hike in daily wages arose due to the heightened consciousness of the workers about their rights and value of their labor, their only asset.

6. *Business and the State Commission*

What is business if it is not the total interdependent commercial activities by people for maintaining their lives? Business and the State Commission monitors the constructive and destructive roles played by these commercial activities to promote a healthy, prosperous and peaceful society after weeding out the negative and destructive activities and their influences on the individuals and society as a whole. Family is the focal point for deciding the good and bad influences of all economic activities. Wealth creation includes education, health, and happy family life apart from other assets.

In India, businessmen do not enjoy a good reputation as Indians generally believe that one cannot make profit in business without being dishonest and indulge in unethical dealings. But, today everybody in India is involved in doing business as he or she is always buying or selling his or her things, ideas, time or service including those meant for free distribution whether for a living or simply for getting richer. From getting a birth certificate for your child to getting a death certificate of your loved one, you have to buy almost all services including those which are otherwise free to you as a citizen of this great country.

In the East, we believe that Earth is our mother and we are her children. As children of one mother, we believe that all have a right to share the land, water and air equitably. In the West, they believe that God had created men and women in His image and that God had given them authority over Earth and its flora and fauna. Unfortunately, a majority of people do not have the opportunity to own land in both East and West. Because, a minority of people has captured all land and would part with it only at prices unaffordable by the deprived majority.

In the West, people who do not have land, have the scope of selling their labor and mental skills at fair prices and earn enough to buy land or a living place. In India even that is not possible. Here, the labor and skills of the deprived in the society have no value in the eyes of those who control the affairs of the nation. Caste system is a major contributing factor for this situation. The people's government that took over reign in 1947 did nothing to change the caste factor influencing the economic affairs of the country.

When the Government fixed prices for the labor and skills of its workers, it failed to fix an equal value for the rest of the workers in the country. Mahatma Gandhi had expressed his view that manual workers and craftsmen should get more or less same pay that was earned by lawyers and similar intellectual workers. His plea was that families of manual workers, craftsmen and intellectual workers have equal needs and therefore both should be compensated in equal manner

In some of the Western countries, manual labor has prices more than the intellectual skills and therefore in such economies, a laborer also can enjoy the comforts such as cars, homes and other luxuries on equal scale with other intellectual workers and business men. Should we in India fix prices of manual labor at par with the intellectual work? While we export our cheap labor to foreign markets and earn valuable foreign exchange, what we do is to negate equal value to our labor in the international market and consequently we acquiesce to same disparities among sections of our own workers. This is because we are still behaving like a feudal society in which class and caste barriers are accepted practices. But, in a democratic republican society, such practices should have been wiped out by and by as, in a republic people are the assets and wealth of the nation. The asset value of all people are equal and equitable in a democratic republic and since future assets of a nation are bounded up in its families, all the families of the poor and rich should be tended and nurtured equitably and this can happen only by paying equitable living wages to the manual and intellectual workers alike.

The Business and the State Commission has the responsibility to redesign the business institution, keeping the Constitutional obligation of making economic, social and political justice the birth right of every citizen of the country in view. It thus, insists on a uniform wage structure throughout the entire spectrum of social structure including the business organizations, for manual and intellectual labor, giving them equal level of purchasing power to lead comfortable lives. The agenda for such a redesign would consist of:

1. *Since people are the wealth of the nation as sovereign, autonomously evolving entities, and since they have the inalienable right given by their Creator to live and pursue happiness, and also since Indian Constitution has given them the right to life, every citizen in India should have the right to earn and possess a certain minimum amount of income that would ensure a decent life, through work, self employment, business or in time of unemployment, through cash subsidy that could fetch a decent life. This should be the attitude of the people who are in business.*

2. *The minimum wages considered in conjunction with the cost of living condition prevailing in India at present, should be upward of Rs.400-500 per day or Rs.12000-15000 per month.*

3. *Per hour cost of labor should be fixed for encouraging part time work across all layers of society and sectors of economy. In times to come in India, part time job culture has to be promoted so that low budget employers and part-time job seekers would be benefited.*

4. *Wearing hat, gloves and gum boots by workers at labor sites should be encouraged so that besides workers getting protection from harsh weather, educated and status conscious people also can enter the manual labor market where serious shortage is felt, without fear of getting their dress soiled and skin darkened. The country would benefit immensely from the additional business and job opportunities that would open up in producing these comfort-enhancing labor accessories.*

5. *India has a very poor business promoting environment. It stands at 132nd position among 185 nations in respect of ease of doing business according to the World Bank Report for 2013. In Singapore which stands at 1st and US which stands at 4th positions, a person can get all permits in few days while in India, it might take months and in certain industries, it might take years. Apart from delays, unhelping attitude of bureaucratic staff is a major disheartening factor faced by a new entrepreneur. This situation has to change as more and more people have to take up entrepreneurship as income source in times to come in India.*

6. *Business institution like all other major institutions, is a major aid to the successful evolution of mankind. It can overwhelm even political, government, religious and mass media institutions adversely and take the evolution of people backward if not guided properly by the government through communication channels of various institutions. There were reports in newspapers*

released on November 2, 2012 about junk foods causing girls to mature at 6 years and boys two years later becoming sexually reproductive. Modern fast foods have the property that can change hormone balance in people who consume them. Traditionally, girls used to become sexually reproductive at the age of 16. But since the introduction of fast foods which have more fat contents, girls and boys started becoming sexually active at lower ages. We have ten year old mothers and twelve year old fathers in our midst now. Tobacco and liquor consumptions cause their own version of adverse influences on genes blocking evolution by years and life-times.

7. *What could be the best business model capable of bringing prosperity to all at total level of the society? Looking at the Mission Statements of the Indian Republic as contained in the Preamble to the Constitution of India, one cannot say that the old and extant economic models would work out a solution for India? Any economic or business model that does not help humanity evolve in the right direction is not the right one for us or any other nation.*

*To fit into the egalitarian goals sought by the Mission Statements in the Constitution of India, a **sarv udai** (sarvodaya or **the rise of all**) model of business needs to be adopted with a mixture of private ownership and cooperative ownership. The example of Amul milk cooperative's success in milk production and distribution is emulative for any type of business that caters to the basic needs of people, including health and education services. Special economic zones which form integral* *parts of modern economies world over, can also be under cooperative ownerships.*

Indian political and economic leaders and experts failed to develop an economic model specifically suitable for India as called for by the objectives of the Republic of India as listed in the Preamble to the Constitution of India. Trained under the British or American systems of education and professional training, Indians largely fail to take note of the special need of India to form its own economic model that could produce an ambience in which all are able to rise in their evolution, meeting their physical, mental and spiritual needs.

8. ***Sarvodaya*** *model of business treats all citizens of India as stake holders of India. Everyone born in India has the birth right to own a house/land in India and those who do not own a plot of land or house, should be in a position to own their own assets with the economic practices that the people and the Government of India adopt. Many a times our sense of welfare limit us from seeing our larger duties towards our fellowmen and women. On October 23, 2012, Chief Minister of Delhi, Sheila Dixit felicitated a group of St Stephen's College students for innovating and making a simple cycle rickshaw convertible into a night shelter for its owner with a six feet bed, mosquito net, FM radio, battery recharging socket and a rack for bottle and magazines. The rear portion of the rickshaw is fitted with folding boards which can be raised to the level of the seat and serving as a bed. The students had studied Delhi's problem of shortage in night shelters for the homeless and came up with the idea*

*of helping rickshaw pullers as they make 30% of the
night-shelter users. The night-shelter rickshaw will cost
Rs.15,000 while a conventional one will cost around
Rs.7000. The students had also made arrangement for
microfinance loans to the rickshaw owners.*

*From the point of sense of welfare, altruism, innovation
and social service, this project merits excellent
commendation and applause. But, looked from the
angle of social responsibility of providing full-fledged
homes to the homeless and from the angle of the problem
of India having the largest number of people defecating
in the open, we would definitely say that the innovation
and the possible business prospects involved in this
project will not add dignity to the Delhi society.*

*The Business and the State Commission is vested with
the responsibility of promoting* **sarvodaya** *model of
business on cooperative basis in neighborhood schools,
colleges, nursing homes, hospitals and infrastructure
including homes for all.*

7. *Ecology and the State Commission*

Perhaps, the world is only learning to recognize the
importance of ecology for including it as a very important
part of good governance. The super storm Sandy that
wreaked havoc on 13 eastern states of USA on October 30,
2012 causing dozens of deaths and damages to properties
to the tune of billions of dollars and shutting out US cities
including New York for almost a week from other parts
of the world, was caused by global warming, according
to environmental scientists and activists. A number of

hurricanes and tsunamis in the recent past have forced world nations to take environment management seriously and give it major attention in day to day governance.

As already mentioned earlier, ecology, economy and ecumenism are all words emanated from the Greek word, **oikomenein** which means the 'entire earth being a home' and these words support each other in their mundane expressions of human activities. Managing the interfaces of economy and home with Mother Earth is not only about managing pollutions and toxicities in air, water and earth but also includes managing the pollutions and toxicities of our social, economic, cultural spaces at individual and collective mental levels. This Commission manages the natural and cultural ecology for the effective management of personal and societal evolution.

Since the modern science approaches environment and ecology through the knowledge at its command, the world over, followers of modern science whose group includes all politicians and economists, solutions to environmental problems are also sought through the limited knowledge of modern science. On one hand, science had advocated the use of so many chemicals and their bonded material such as pesticides, fertilizers, plastic and polythene products and on the other, the same science has now discovered that the use of many of these chemicals and its bonded material are hazardous for the environment.

While we are familiar with the pollution caused by chemicals to earth, water, fire and air, we are not familiar with the pollution caused to ether, the fifth of the classic elements recognized and respected by all cultures from ancient times.

Modern science may not approve of the belief which almost all ancient cultures embraced, that the prototypes of all manifested creations have beginning in etheric world and then they proceed to express themselves in the physical world of earth, water, fire and air. Ancient wisdom suggests that there is a certain limit to the permissible level of pollution in the visible world of earth, water, fire and air. Beyond that, the etheric world and its laws will react, resist and repulse or reorganize the imbalances in the lower elements of earth, water, fir and air, caused by the pollutants. The methods of balancing act by the etheric world and its laws might become too much for us, the feeble earth-lings to deal with at times, especially when these balancing acts are through tsunamis, super storms, earth quakes and volcanic eruptions!

Muslim clerics in Arab world attributed the destruction by hurricane Sandy in the US to the hate films distributed by evangelical Christians in that country. Though it sounds a bit silly and supercilious, if one considers hatred or hateful thought as a form of heat energy, its capacity to contribute to the global warming, cannot be ruled out. What we read in scriptures of the East and West as wraths of God, inflicted in the form of earth quakes, floods and volcano eruptions as punishments for the sins of mankind, are really, effects of violation of Nature's laws of evolution. Since all sinful actions are effects of thoughts of negative character capable of interfering with the laws of etheric world where all prototypes of the physical world exists, scripture writers deliberately created fear in the minds of people to dissuade them from violating laws of the etheric world. For, beyond a certain tolerance level, Nature will take steps to restore the lost balance by releasing out all negatively reacted energies through floods, earthquakes, volcanic eruptions and storms.

In our idea of being Indians of a proud past, productive present and a prosperous future, we cannot accommodate the idea of being the owners of a highly polluted nation. Nor are we willing to accommodate the thought in our mind that the India in the making, should have serious ecological problems. But the reality is that India is a highly polluted country. Its soil, water bodies and atmosphere are contaminated much above the permissible levels.

As mentioned elsewhere in this book, half of India's people do not own toilets and defecate in open fields, roads and railway land stretches. The Bhopal gas tragedy is still a shame for India even after 28 years. About 346 metric tons of toxic waste is lying within the premises of the erstwhile Union Carbide India Ltd (UCIL) at Bhopal where the worst-ever industrial disaster had taken place on the intervening night of December 2-3, 1984. A discussion by Indian authorities with a German firm for disposal of this toxic material in September 2012, failed to yield results. According to government data, over Rs 3,000 crore has been given as compensation in 5,295 cases of death, 4,902 cases of permanent disability, 5,27,894 cases of minor injury and 35,455 cases related to temporary disability due to the gas tragedy.

While Bhopal gas tragedy is a sign of India's low level reaction and reasoning towards pollution pain suffered by common man, many such cases are piling before us from Kerala, Orissa and Punjab on pesticides induced deaths, deformities and disagreement of pesticide companies to stop production and distribution of chemicals which threaten many lives of people.

The Comptroller and Auditor General of India had tabled its Performance Audit of Government on Water Pollution in India in Parliament on December 16, 2011, in which it said the government had given low priority to water pollution issues. It said the resources available for prevention of pollution, treatment of polluted water and ecological restoration of polluted water bodies were woefully inadequate. The audit further said that despite 26 years of implementation of various programs to control pollution, water in major rivers was critically polluted. The situation was particularly alarming in 14 major and 55 minor and several hundred small rivers as 90% of the millions of litres of untreated sewage and industrial and agricultural waste was dumped into them.

According to the CAG, with the exception of Ganga in certain stretches, all the other rivers test-checked by it i.e., Ganga, Yamuna, Gomti, Godavari, Musi, Cauvery, Cooum, Mahananda, Khan, Kshipra, Vaigai, Chambal, Rani Chu, Mandovi, Sabarmati, Subarnarekha, Bhadra/Tungabhadra, Pennar, Pamba, Betwa, Krishna, Sutlej etc., continued to have high levels of organic pollution, and low level of oxygen availability for aquatic organisms. The water was infected by disease causing bacteria, protozoa and viruses which have fecal origin.

India's air is the world's unhealthiest, according to a report in the New York Times of February 1, 2012 by Heather Timons and Malavika Vyawahare. According to the report, India has the worst air pollution in the entire world, beating China, Pakistan, Nepal and Bangladesh, according to a study released during this year's World Economic Forum in Davos. Of the 132 countries whose environments were surveyed,

India ranked last in the 'Air (effects on human health)' ranking. The annual study, the *Environmental Performance Index*, was written by environmental research centers at Yale and Columbia universities with assistance from dozens of outside scientists. The study used satellite data to measure air pollution concentrations.

"When it comes to overall environment, India ranked among the world's worst performers, at 125th position out of the 132 nations, beating only Kuwait, Yemen, South Africa, Kazakhstan, Uzbekistan, Turkmenistan and Iraq. Neighboring Pakistan, in contrast, ranked 120th and Bangladesh was listed as No. 115 on overall environment," said the New York Times report. India's high levels of fine particulate matter are one of the major factors contributing to the country's abysmal air quality. Levels of so-called PM 2.5, (the 2.5 micron size of the particulates) are nearly five times the threshold where they become unsafe for human beings.

Particulate matter is one of the leading causes of acute lower respiratory infections and cancer. The World Health Organization found that Acute Respiratory Infections were one of the most common causes of deaths in children under 5 in India, and contributed to 13% in-patient deaths in pediatric wards in India.

Waste disposal and recycling is at the lowest ebb in India and the level of interest or inertia shown by general public is simply pathetic. Civic education in India seems to have made no headway even after 66 years of independent republican status it boast of. Whether it is household waste, or municipal or hospital, India's urban road sides are increasingly being used for their safe storage as if Indian municipal authorities cherish the belief that an already sick society could not be made more sick by anything let alone, urban waste.

The Ecology and State Commission demands urgent action by the people and the legally constituted bodies to do the following exercises:

1. *Since pollution levels in all the five elemental realms have reached the dangerous tolerant marks, the citizens at total level of the population have to get up from their slumber and start doing corrective actions to stem the tide of the oncoming mass destructions caused by climate change. The governments at central, state and local levels must alert citizens.*

2. *Action groups must be formed in all Panchayat and Municipality Wards across the country for effective handling of pollution management with respect to air, water and soil contamination by pesticides, vehicle and industrial fumes and human fecal matter.*

3. *For effective disposal of household waste, every single family must be held responsible through residents welfare associations to send out the household wastes in properly closed bags for depositing at the bin assigned by the Municipality.*

4. *Residents Welfare Associations must be empowered to monitor the Municipality's effectiveness in managing the waste disposal from their residential areas including those wastes from hospitals and food processing units of both vegetarian and non-vegetarian categories. Ward level waste collection centers must be equipped with staff and machineries to sort out and cinder and incinerate*

5. *Every town and city in India should have adequate number of treatment plants to process sewage and*

industrial effluents generated in each of them. Similarly every village/Panchayat should have enough plants to treat its human and industrial effluents.

6. *Every village, town and city in India must be made responsible to see that no sewage and industrial effluent is dumped into Indian rivers without treating them. Municipal Commissioners and Panchayat Secretaries should be made responsible for ensuring this.*

7. *Since environmental problem is a life and death problem for the citizens, Government of India must spend more funds on research of making pesticides and fertilizers that are harmless to soil and human life streams and also for making organic farming a widespread practice.*

8. *Since water scarcity is a major ecological problem, every Panchayat and Municipal Ward in India must take up rain harvesting on priority, without wasting any more valuable time. Also, since rain and trees are intricately related to each other, tree plantation must be taken on priority by every Panchayat and Municipal Ward for inducing clouds to give more rains.*

8. *Infrastructure and the State Commission*

An infrastructure, in ideology is the structure which carries on it a super-structure or in other words, it is the base structure on which the main structure of a facility is built. In technology, physical infrastructure really are those facilities which are basic to the successful functional existence of a larger facility or a project. The health, optimal function and long life of the larger facility or project depend on the optimal strength, size and long life of the infrastructure. The successful functional existences of both the larger facility or project and their supporting basic infrastructure are first conceived and established as ideas or ideological structure. So, what could be the infrastructure on which the super-structure Indian Republic has been erected? Think about it and in the meantime, we will discuss what is the current social perception and mental images of people about infrastructure.

Currently, what passes off as infrastructure in the present socio-economic-political nomenclature mainly comprises the land, roads, drainage, sewer lines, water pipe lines, power plants, telecommunication lines, manufacturing projects, highways, airports, sea ports, dams, and a host of similar facilities that keep a nation in perpetual movement either in forward or backward evolutionary direction. These facilities are also aptly called the infrastructure by corporate entities because, some or many of them are basic to any project they handle. But, in our *sarvodaya good governance model*, infrastructure would mean much more than these!

We have already seen in our discussions so far, that the Indian Republic had a grand vision at the time of its formation and this vision had been captured in the Preamble to the Constitution of India in the form of Mission Statements, the Republic of India had to achieve. In fact, we the people of India had formulated the vision comprising the missions of i) constituting India into a sovereign, socialist, secular and democratic India; ii) securing social, economic and political justice; liberty of thought, expression, belief, faith and worship; equality of status and of opportunity; and iii) promoting fraternity among all citizens, assuring the dignity of the individual and the unity and the integrity of the nation.

Our missions in the Constitution of India are the design criteria for building a healthy, prosperous and peaceful nation out of our being Indians. Yes, we are building India into a healthy, prosperous and peaceful Republic using the design criteria given in the Constitution. The Republic of India is the idea of a cooperative self sufficient habitat. The Indian Republic is the super-structure standing on the various infrastructure in the various states forming the federal India.

The Preamble to the Constitution of India contains the super-structure of the Republic of India and the infrastructure on which the Republic should stand, in ideal form. The ideology of the nature and structure of the Indian Republic as contained in the Preamble to the Constitution, while being transferred into physical form, should have been supported with infrastructure of corresponding ideological nature and structure for effective expression and experiential satisfaction. This has not happened. Why we suffer today is because of the mismatch between the selected infrastructure of the administration, judiciary and police of the British feudal ideological system and the Indian Republican ideology.

The ideological super-structure of the Indian Republic of sovereign, socialist, secular, democratic nature should have been built on ideological infrastructure of matching sovereign, socialist, secular and democratic nature. Instead, our founding fathers the Constituent Assembly had grafted the feudal infrastructure from the British feudal ideology of the savage variety that was employed in ruling the Indian colony for more than two hundred years, onto the republican format of the free India. This aberrant behavior of the founding fathers was a proof of what Nehru stated in the Discovery of India that the people from the British feudal

185

society of the savage variety who came and ruled India had succeeded in creating a feudal middle class in India and the same middle class wanted only to send the British out of India and not their 'crushing structure of government.'

Physical infrastructure systems mandated by the ideological sovereign, socialist, secular, democratic republic of India as expressed in the Preamble to the Constitution of India would require us to create republican infrastructure of administration, police and judiciary at total population level, through the villages, districts, towns and cities. Whereas the British colonial government in India and its staff of both European and Indian origin were serving their masters in England with the support of the self-serving middle class section of the Indian society, the Republican democratic, secular, socialist and sovereign government of independent India would serve the people of India with staff and supporting institutions trained to love and help one another at the total population level. Because, the difference between feudal and democratic ideologies is essentially of self loving and self serving values whereas the democratic republican ideology is and should be absolutely of egalitarian values respecting the sovereignty of every individual for autonomous evolution with a fraternal love for one another irrespective of class, caste and creed.

We the people of India should be following the *sarvodaya* model of good governance as contained in the Preamble to the Constitution of India, with some urgency of course, to avoid an avalanche of anti-government displeasure in the country:

1. *Every Panchayat and Municipality Ward in the country should have a development office manned by an IAS officer trained not to collect revenue and control through feudal-fascist force of the police and judiciary but to monitor the development need of the people at total level of the population and then plan, obtain financial resources and implement schemes and services on fast track action mode.*

2. *It is his duty to promote fraternity among citizens assuring the dignity of the individuals and the unity and integrity of the nation through people's councils of all-caste, all class and all-religious participation. Where there is fraternal fervor for each other in a community, there will be less chance for violence against each other.*

3. *He will ensure that every family has sufficient income to lead a comfortable life through jobs that pay living wages, trades and agriculture activities. Paying the living wages is an absolute must, for all labor whether skilled or unskilled or handicrafts works. Without a living wage-system in the country, the ideological system of social, economic and political justice will be naught and the Constitutional mandate will be nullified and Republican super-structure will crumble down. But, since India does not have a living wage system of infrastructure so far, the Republic that we the people dreamed had not yet been erected. It is the feudal middle class of India which claim that India is a Republic. Without a living wage system at total level of the population, the claim of sovereignty, socialism and secularism is hollow.*

4. *The Indian penal code system should be thoroughly revised to fit into the democratic republican objectives of the Indian Republic. The one in use was made for*

running the colonial British government. Since a majority of political representatives in Parliament and the officers in administrative and judicial systems are from the feudal minded middle class, the revision job of the penal codes should be referred to the people's councils at Panchayat and Municipal Wards level.

5. *All disputes among the citizens should be first referred to and settled by the people's councils amicably, keeping the Constitutional spirit and obligation to promote fraternity among citizens keeping their dignity and the unity and integrity of the nation. Only crimes like murders and disputes with the government should go to courts where keeping the Constitutional obligation of promoting fraternity among citizens, no cases should be pending for more than ten months. For, beyond such a long period of ten months, animosities and acrimonies will fluster and flourish between the families and their supporters of the litigants of both accused and victims.*

6. *Every Ward in the Panchayats and Municipalities should have a police station and police staff should be from both sexes in equal number and of minimum college level education and trained in the multi-religious-cultural ethos of the country. The police should be made accountable to the people's council and be a friend and counselor to the people.*

7. *Every Ward in the Panchayats and Municipalities should have schools of primary and secondary levels and colleges of both scholarly and professional varieties. Similarly, every Ward in the Panchayats and Municipalities should have nursing homes and hospitals in both allopathic and Indian medicine systems like Ayurveda, Yoga, Naturopathy, Homoeopathy and*

> *Unani. Health service and doctors' services should be made available to people at their homes on 24x7 basis.*
>
> 8. *Every family in India should be able to own houses or land to build houses and these must be made a fundamental right. All such houses or lands given to families should be of such standard and dignity as that of the middle class. The living wage system should be such that people are able to afford middle class homes and assets like transport vehicles. All major infrastructure such as the roads, parks, markets, railways, waterways, dams and irrigational projects, industrial plants, airports, sea ports and other similar facilities should be directed to the welfare of the families at total level of the society irrespective of class, caste, and gender barriers.*

9. *Religion and the State Commission*

Religions are essentially institutions for managing the evolution of their members towards their successful and happy living. This Commission looks after the interfaces of all religions in the Indian Republic and ensures their cooperative contribution to the well-being of the Republic, especially in tune with the Constitutional mandate to promote FRATERNITY among the citizens, assuring their individual dignity and the integrity of the nation.

In our *sarvodaya* model of good governance, religion as an institution is an aid to the evolution of the people in the right direction and in the right measure. The English word 'religion' has its root in the Latin language and the Latin root means 'to bind.' It has nothing to do with spirituality except that as one becomes more evolved, he or she becomes more conscious of the oneness of humanity in terms of its origin in the spiritual realm, the quantum level existence of the Universe.

In the ancient periods, leaders of highly evolved minds used to gather people in monastic or temple communities and bind them on certain rites and doctrines directed towards their common physical, mental and spiritual development, thus taking them onwards on the path of evolution. This allegiance to a particular discipline set by sages and seers was actually known as religion.

Secularism, on the other hand, we have seen in previous sections of this book, is the spiritual oneness of a generation with respect for all religions. Secularism is about being one with all religions while being a member of a particular religion or an athiest. Because, it ignores parts and prefers the whole! To bring the objectives of the Constitution of India into fruition, people in the Government need not be religious or belonging to a particular religion. But, without being spiritual, i.e. feeling oneness with the larger society, people in the Government cannot bring the Mission Statements in the Preamble to the Constitution into reality.

A minister, an MP, an IAS officer or an employee has to be one in spirit with the people of his/her country for him to think and act benevolently for them. He has to be secular. He or she may be staunch follower of a religion and may not be one in spirit with his/her country and men and women. But if he/she being a staunch follower of a particular religion and then thinks and acts as one in spirit with the country-men, then he/she is secular and spiritual.

We have religion in our model as the science of evolution. Yes, every religion in its pure form is the repository of treatises on the science of evolution and the cosmic unity of life. If we examine the scriptures of religions, they may look like children's stories or so called myths. But, if we approach them with relevant clues, they will reveal wonderful facts about the Universe and its evolution. Actually these mythological stories are facts and figures regarding the past, present and future evolution of the Universe.

Take for instance the ten avatars of God in the Hindu scriptures. Matsya or the fish, Koorma or tortoise, Varaha or the pig, Narasimha or the half-man and half-animal, Vaman or the dwarf, Parasuram or the hunter, Sri Rama or the fully evolved man at physical, mental and spiritual levels, Krishna or the divine man, Buddha or the cosmically enlightened man and finally Kalki the ascended man, are all the stages of life on Earth through which the entire human race has to pass through. In the Old Testament Bible, which is common to Jews, Christians and Muslims, the one-week creation story is in fact, the evolution story of the Earth and its life streams. In the books of Daniel, Ezekiel and Revelation in the Bible reference is found in allegorical forms to the future of Earth on the evolutionary journey.

Creator reveals himself or herself in cycles of periods of evolution. A careful scrutiny of religious scriptures reveals to us an intelligent plan present in them to guide us on the eternal verity that we are children of one central source; that as spirits from that source we are evolving along with the Universe which also had come from that central source and that our only qualifying sign of our evolution forward is our love for one another as children of one father. As these eternal verities are presented in symbolic stories, many of us enjoy the drama of the stories and fail to see the symbols.

Modern science also recognizes the fact that life started in the oceans, represented here by the fish. Then, life started on land as well. Tortoise represents the amphibian life. Pig represents a developed mammalian animal. Then men appear in half human and half animal stage but giants. The dwarf stage represents the shrinkage of human stature from that of the giant to that of present human stature. Parasuram was the next stage in man's evolution. The present stage of human race is passing through the Sri Ram era. Lord Krishna's, Lord Buddha's and Kalki's stages are yet to come to the human race and earth as a whole.

Kalki is the stage of the earth and its life streams becoming fully spiritualized and ready for merger into the source of creation, the Creator's consciousness or the causeless Cause. Then after a night of rest by the Creator another round of creation will follow, as per Hindu scriptural texts.

Egyptian, Mayan and European mythologies also more or less corroborate the Hindu metaphysical stories on evolution. According to these, the earth will pass through, Jupiter, Venus and Vulcan Periods of astral or etheric existence for earth and its life streams. Earth is in the middle of its current Period known as the Earth Period. Out of the 4.32 billion years assigned to the present round of Creation, almost half remains to be lived out, according to both Eastern and Western monastic sciences.

Using Religion and the State Commission of the *sarvodaya* good governance model, a republican government, especially equipped with the Constitutional mandate *to promote fraternity* among its citizens, could produce the synergy required for a republic to manage the evolution of its people at total level of the population. The oneness and unity among people at total population level which religions failed to create because of the exclusiveness and absolutism crept into them as they grew in number can be recreated and spread across the whole nation at total level of the population by our government using the republican structure under its command:

1. *The Ward Councils of all Panchayats and Municipalities throughout the country are constituted with representatives from all major religions in the region or state.*

2. *All development issues planned and executed in the Wards by the Ward Councils are thus endorsed and encouraged by the representatives of all major religions. This will encourage not only the disparate religious groups to unite themselves on common platform, but also to rediscover their lost souls of Universal Oneness and Love which are the attributes required for running a republic.*

3. *Vasudhaiva Kutumbakam or 'the entire world is one family' is a concept taken from Maha Upanishad(ayam bandhurayam neti ganana laghuchetasam udaracharitanam tu vasudhaiva kutumbakam—small men discriminate saying: One is a relative; the other is a stranger. For those who live magnanimously the entire world constitutes but a family.) Though this is a basic concept of Hindu religion, fundamentally all religions are based on the oneness of God the father and the oneness among His children, the members of the entire*

human race. Since republican democracy is best served by the concept 'vasudhaiva kutumbakam,' the Ward Councils plan and execute their development projects based on this concept.

4. *We should review this situation and rebuild our relation with our neighbors based on this eternal verity. Around the key maxim, 'vasudhaiva kutumbakam', India could build its foreign policy and win not only hearts of other nations but become a model for other nations.*

5. *Around India, we have Islamic, Buddhist and Hindu nations as our neighbors and with them our relations are not in the best of forms in spite of having a civilizational history of viewing the world through the prism of 'vasudhaiva kutumbakam.' It is high time that we review this situation.*

6. *Indian caste system is nothing less than racism of its own kind. Instead of building a caste-less society, we have been strengthening caste consciousness over the years since adopting a Constitution that sought a caste-less society. Religion and the State Commission has the responsibility of managing our transition to a caste-less Indian society.*

7. *This Commission also oversees Inter-Faith harmony being maintained at all costs.*

8. *A religion engaged only in fulfilling membership obligations without social service irrespective of religious, caste and class labels, cannot be a true religion. Therefore, every religion in the country is encouraged to engage in social service and uplift activities in every Ward.*

10. *Relief and Rehabilitation and State Commission*

What is the need of this Commission in a good governance model? Many of you might have confronted this question at the sight of this Commission name. The answer is very simple. If you happen to visit a nation and its society at the height of its good luck of having a good life for all its citizens, you may still meet with people of four types needing relief and rehabilitation help. Who are they? One, people affected by accidents and natural calamities. Two, people who are victims of drugs and alcoholic abuse. Three, people who are victims of incurable diseases such as HIV/AIDS, chronic anemia and cancer. Four, people with permanent disability in vision, hearing, speech and use of hands and legs. But, since we are in India, we will have many more types of needy people afflicted by chronic hunger.

In India we have two Government bodies working in the fields of rehabilitation and disaster management known as the Rehabilitation Council of India(RCI) and the National Disaster Management Authority(NDMA). Both are signs of growing awareness of the need to integrate rehabilitation management with the country's development management so that the body of the Indian society will be kept whole continuously, in spite of the occasional pathological states it might incur.

"The Rehabilitation Council of India (RCI) was set up as a registered society in 1986. On September, 1992 the RCI Act was enacted by Parliament and it became a Statutory Body on 22 June 1993. The Act was amended by Parliament in 2000 to make it more broad-based. The mandate given to RCI is to regulate and monitor services given to persons with disability, to standardize syllabi and to maintain a Central Rehabilitation Register of all qualified professionals and personnel working in the field of Rehabilitation and Special Education. The Act also prescribes punitive action against unqualified persons delivering services to persons with disability," says the website of RCI.

An approach paper on NDMA website reads: "Till recently, the approach to Disaster Management has been reactive and relief centric. A paradigm shift has now taken place at the national level from the relief centric syndrome to holistic and integrated approach with emphasis on prevention, mitigation and preparedness. These efforts are aimed to conserve developmental gains as also minimize losses to lives, livelihood and property.

A typical Disaster Management continuum, comprising six elements i.e., Prevention, Mitigation and Preparedness in pre-disaster phase, and Response, Rehabilitation and Reconstruction in post-disaster phase, defines the complete approach to Disaster Management." The NDMA was constituted in 2005.

Though these two progressive outfits seem to give us reasons to celebrate at the outset, the truth that these were instituted at the instance of UN and not born out of our republican consciousness of oneness amongst the citizens, takes away whatever feelings of pride and joy one ought to have genuinely felt. There are many orphanages and distress homes for women and children across the country run by Government and we all are familiar with the pathetic conditions of them. The care and concern one ought to feel for one's fellow citizens in a democracy are a rare sight in our society even after our commitment with ourselves to do so through the Mission Statements of the Indian Republic, we have made in 1950.

The Relief and Rehabilitation & the State Commission is all about state's responsibility in providing relief and rehabilitation to the last citizen of the country who has no means to support himself or herself for leading a decent life. A citizen could be in a pathetic condition due to a variety of reasons. Disability from birth or accident or disease; natural calamities, drug or alcohol abuse, domestic violence, social rejection after prison terms or drug rehabilitation, inability to treat life threatening diseases due to extreme poverty and inability to fight hunger and starvation. India abounds in these.

"So long as the millions live in hunger and ignorance, I hold every man a traitor, who having been educated at their expense, pays not the least heed to them," said Swami Vivekananda and we, who endorse the missions of the Indian Republic as enshrined in the Preamble to the Constitution of India, are apt to be the ones whom Vivekananda described as traitors. The Bhopal Gas tragedy scam and the lakhs of citizens rendered physical and neurological wrecks by it, unable to lead a quality life and the lakhs of victims of the Narmada Dam resettlement scam still fighting for legitimate rehabilitation are examples of how insensitive our people in government functions are towards their fellow men and women.

If we as Indian citizens wish to enjoy our idea of being Indians, and if we really care how our India in the making should be, then we have to have certain minimum number of actions in making the institution of relief and rehabilitation in India responsive to the people in times of their need.

1.   *The People's Council in every Panchayat and Municipality Ward must be empowered to deal with all types of rehabilitation measures including those under RCI and NDMA. The federal government should treat all relief and rehabilitation issues from the point of view of Indian society being one organic whole and the suffering of one individual is like the suffering of a part on the body of the Indian society.*

2.   *Looking at the missions of the Indian Republic in the Preamble to the Constitution of India, the first major rehabilitation area in India is the housing needs of people who are not in a position to own a house of their own. The People's Council in every Ward in the country must be empowered to make sure that no one in its Ward goes without a roof over his or her head.*

3.   *The second major area of attention is the hungry in the country. The People's Council in every Ward must be empowered to ensure that none in its Ward goes hungry to bed in the night. As hunger caused by poverty is the most debilitating dis-easing force facing a man or woman, the People's Council must ensure that every house-hold has the purchasing power to buy foods that give enough nutrients needed by its members. Where there is such purchasing power missing, the People's Council ensures that the government supplies such foods free.*

4.   *Religion and language are causes of riots in Indian society. When deliberate peacekeeping and fraternity*

promotion fail in our country, riots are prone to break out in our society. Ward-wise rehabilitation systems must be in place to deal with such situations. The People's Councils are responsible to set up such systems under the disaster management regime.

5. *The People's Council in every Ward in the country should have response systems ready for reaching support to orphans and lonely people of all ages and sexes. Where these hapless are poor and deprived of personal wealth or assets, the state should take care of them in orphanages and old age homes built and maintained by state-supported agencies.*

6. *Victims of drugs abuse, HIV/AIDS and long prison life, generally do not get acceptance when they come out of their captivity of either drug habit or prisons and in such cases, Ward-wise arrangement must be in place for accommodating them and rehabilitating them with jobs, shelters and personal security.*

7. *In India many poor cannot afford costly medical services and die unattended by fellowmen and women and authorities. This situation has to go and state should come forward with help for them. Every Ward must have systems coming for heir help.*

8. *The health and harmony level of a society or nation depend on the willingness and preparedness of that society to meet all relief and rehabilitation needs of its house-holds and members. To make all people responsible for each other and each for all others in a republic, so that the republic resound with the hopes and joys of its people, the institution of government of that republic has to create the necessary culture. To create a culture that will sustain the joys and hopes of people of a nation, its government has to produce the*

relevant communication and media setup. Not only the mass media, but the key institutions including the education institution, have to be used as special media besides their assigned functions. The Relief and Rehabilitation and State Commission, plays the role of creating the culture we talked about.

11. *Mass Media and the State Commission*

The mass media is in our *sarvodaya* good governance model as a crucial institution, in just the manner we have included the other key institutions for their role in managing the evolution of people towards a successful living style, which in turn will become epigenetic in nurturing a human culture that will take the humanity to its pinnacle of evolution, enjoying divine perfection in body, mind and soul while celebrating zero level of violence, lies, fraudulent practices and the ever presence of health, prosperity and peace at 100% population level. Though mass media is not a formal institution like family, health, education etc, considering the primal importance it occupies in modern society, we need to give more attention to it in making it a functionally more useful institution in spite of all its negative influences.

Former supreme court judge, Justice Markandey Katju, the present chairman of the Press Council of India(2012-2015), has been very bold in declaring Indian media's negative roles outbalancing its positive roles, in many of his speeches and articles. According to him, Indian media are at fault with 3 sins. One, high focus on frivolous topics such as cricket, films, business tycoons and entertainment with very little coverage on India's caste system, poverty, shortages of hospitals, schools and housing, sickness and malnutrition faced by almost 80% of its citizens. Two, the media divide society into religious, linguistic and regional groups with sensational twists given to news instead of treating the news in terms of the need of the Indian Republic to be united and thriving in its diversity. Three, the Indian media fail to elevate the mental level of people with reportage on the need to be modern and broad minded but, instead, media thrive on coverage of superstitions, fanatic and feudal practices of the affluent.

Justice Katju wrote to the Government of India asking to bring the electronic media and print media together but, according to a news report of November 15. 2012, the Government had refused to heed to Justice Katju's proposal. The broadcast media was already being controlled by the News Broadcasting Standards Authority (NBSA), a self-regulatory mechanism of the News Broadcasters' Association, chaired by the late Chief Justice of India, J.S. Verma and the Broadcasting Content Complaints Council (BCCC) headed by A.P. Shah, former Chief Justice of the Delhi High Court.

The BCCC was a self-regulatory body constituted by the Indian Broadcasters' Association and entertained complaints from viewers. The electronic media regulatory bodies are headed by a former Chief Justice of the Supreme Court of India and a former Chief Justice of the Delhi High Court respectively, thus *commanding* enough respect not only from Government corridors but also from legal fraternity. Though Justice Katju's proposal had lot of wisdom, the broadcast media did not want the high wage structure dictated by the Press Council controlled journalists wage board to disturb the profit making electronic media to face the hardship of some of the loss making print media. The Indian Newspapers Society (INS) which fought in vain against the journalists wage-board's decision to revise working journalists' wages without reference to the financial health of the newspaper companies, also had objected to Justice Katju's proposal.

When late Vasant Sathe, while he was being the Information and Broadcasting Minister in Indira Gandhi's cabinet, had put forward an idea of starting an all India news-digest to high-light the development works taking place in a vast country such as India but seldom reported in news media. Indira Gandhi's perception also was that mass media showed little interest in the good works taking place in the course of the Indian Republic's march forward.

But, what Justice Markandey Katju and many others such as Anna, Kejriwal, and Swami Ramdev want the media to do was to cover what the Government was not doing and what was not happening which ought to have happened on the basis of the Mission Statements in the Preamble to the Constitution of India. This is the focus the Mass Media and the State Commission wishes to have in shaping the idea of being Indians and the making of a resplendent India:

1.   *The relief and rehabilitation needs of the Indian society is so huge that a deliberate **culture of care and concern** for one another calls for urgent attention from all of us. In today's world, media have high contents of educative material both of good and bad varieties. Practically, the print and electronic media including the Internet is available to people from the age of as early as 5 years. We must persuade content creators to bring out the **care and concern** contents through children's*

cartoon films and comics magazines as designed programs.

2. Since all self regulating ethical and moral consciousness are formed mainly in families, deliberate designed communication programs need to be created and transmitted through both electronic and print media to families for children and parents. Parents are the first teachers of children and this ability needs to be built in parents through electronic and print media. **Family Communication** has to be developed as a separate stream of communication discipline. Mass media and the educational institutions of schools and colleges should participate jointly in this project.

3. **Education Communication** is already a formal institution and apart from the set of knowledge and skills imparted through the schools and colleges at present, a more streamlined set of information on citizenship training and partnering republic building had to be part of educational contents. Mass media should share **Education Communication** for both students and adult public at large.

4. **Health Communication** need more and urgent attention to widen its scope to cover mass media and general educational institutions apart from the health institutes and medical colleges. Contents of **Health Communication** flowing through health institutions, family institutions, educational institutions, mass media and inter-personal communication should have central theme of **care and concern** for one another.

5. **Business Communication** is receiving maximum attention from people in both traditional and modern sections of society, with the deliberate intent of being influenced by the charms of business institution.

Business communication flowing through channels of all key institutions of society lacks sensitiveness to its role as a major aid to the successful evolution of people towards attaining health, prosperity and peace in their lives. We have to introduce more **care and concern** for one another in contents of **Business Communication.**

6. **Religious Communication**, one of the major mass communication processes that have influenced culture formation and identities throughout the world from ancient times, has come to focus more on self-perpetuation efforts of religions, than their spiritual contents of **care and concern** for people irrespective of their various identities. Mass media, both independent and religiously affiliated need to be educated on the Mission Statements of the Indian Republic and Religion and the State Commission has to respond to this need.

7. **Interpersonal Communication** processes in a democratic republic and a feudal society are different like day is different from night. The Constitutional compulsions for a casteless and classless society demanded that we nurture a communication practice among the citizens so that we get the culture which prepare us for casteless and classless society. Unfortunately, so far, we as a nation have not tried anything of that sort but the time has come now for us to initiate steps in that direction. Many of our institutions are still steeped in feudal mind set and the resultant interpersonal communication processes are quite antagonistic to the spirit of democracy and republicanism.

8. National and International Communication practices in Indian society should be the harmonic blend of the communication practices we have narrated in the

preceding seven paragraphs, containing seven major steps of action.

12. *Government and the State Commission*

In our *sarvodaya good governance model,* government and state are two distinct entities. State is the collective will of the people expressed in the Constitution of a country or a republic, especially in our case, in the Preamble to the Constitution of India. In a way, we can say that we are the state, because, state is the collective will or consciousness of our being for designing our future on the path of evolution towards successful living. The government is the central, coordinating institution or social system to direct the working of all other social institutions or systems and natural systems for the collective evolution of people towards healthy, prosperous, happy and peaceful living.

A good government is distinguished by the good governance designs employed in managing the various social and natural systems for achieving collective prosperity, health and peace at total level or 100% level of the population. Bad government is likewise distinguished by the bad governance designs used for managing the various social and natural systems for achieving collective health and prosperity first for the influential sections of the society and then in halting steps for the left-out masses and never achieves the 100% population level.

Where do we stand on the scale of good governance and bad governance? Obviously on the wanting side of the bad governance designs and the scantily achieved social goals. Here, we have to take a hard look at the state of affairs in our nation. Remember, we have set out on our journey to find out what constitutes the idea of being Indians and what constitutes the making of India. We all are familiar with the awarding system employed by society from the very early stage of its evolution. Good work was hailed and rewarded and bad works hated and punished. But, though we are given bad governance results by our governance personnel including, the government workers, the legislators and the ministers, we cannot award them punishment. If we thought that we would punish them through 5-yearly elections, that too becomes ineffective because, the nexus between the feudal, family owned and self-aggrandizing leaders-led Indian political parties and caste and class ridden and favor mongering electorates make it impossible to throw away the albatross of the power-hungry corrupt governments. As for government workers, less said is better for our peace of mind. They are not serving the people of India. They are serving the government of India which is designed on the pattern of a cloned model of colonial government by yoking the feudal, colonial systems of administration, judiciary and police with the parliamentary legislature.

According to a news report in the Times of India of April 15, 2011, activist Dev Ashish Bhattacharya filed an RTI application on February 2, 2009 with the Election Commission seeking details of duties, responsibilities and accountability of MPs and MLAs. The commission replied that it was not concerned with information sought and it had no such information. On an appeal, the commission's appellate authority ruled that the query should have been transferred to the ministry of parliamentary affairs and ministry of law and justice.

The Lok Sabha secretariat said on June 3, 2009 that there was no provision either in the Constitution or the Rules of Procedure and Conduct of Business in Lok Sabha defining duties and responsibilities of members of Parliament or through which the accountability can be fixed on non-performing MPs. The activist had gone through the states' replies on the MLAs' duties and found that they also repeated the same replies of the Election Commission of India and the Lok Sabha secretariat.

India's political parties have lost legitimacy in looking after the interests of the people as they have failed to work for the objectives of the Indian Republic laid out in the Preamble to the Constitution of India. I know, you may be shocked by this statement but, can you honestly say they are following the Mission Statements enshrined in the Preamble to the Constitution? I have gone through the objectives of the major political parties and found that not one party had among their objectives, the fulfillment of the Mission Statements of the Indian Republic contained in the Preamble. A semblance of closeness to the Mission Statements of the Republic of India, was found only in the objectives of the BSP or Bahujan Samaj Party led by Mayawati.

Rahul Gandhi who was elevated from the post of General Secretary of Congress Party to that of Vice President on January 19, 2013 admitted to his party workers the next day that there was no laws and rules in his party and yet it won elections just because his party had the DNA of India. He lamented the highly centralized hierarchical functioning of Congress alienating the ranks and files howsoever knowledgeable they were in the development of the nation! Since Congress ruled India most of the 65 years after its freedom, one could imagine the effect of its oligarchic rule as Rahul Gandhi had admitted.

Rahul assured his party workers that he will work fearlessly for a change and bring in decentralized democratic working laws and directions. In 1985, Rajiv Gandhi also indicated radical changes in the working of his party and government. But not much happened. In the entrenched feudal oligarchic set up of the governance structures established in the pattern existed in the colonial days, any party change towards democratic functioning may not bring in intended results in national development, unless these colonial feudal governance structures are changed into republican ones and sooner it is done better for the nation.

In a study titled, 'Incumbents and Criminals in the Indian National Legislature,' jointly conducted by Toke Aidt of University of Cambridge, UK, Miriam A. Golden of University of California at Los Angeles and Devesh Tiwari of University of California at San Diego, on trends of Indian political parties selecting candidates with criminal charges, based on the 2004 and 2009 general elections to Indian Parliament, the shocking results were that a quarter of the MPs elected to the Lok Sabha had criminal charges which they themselves have declared in affidavits submitted before the Election Commission, prior to the elections. Their study results which were submitted to various scientific and professional forums during 2009-2011 at international level, have established the fact that Indian political parties preferred to nominate a candidate with criminal records because of his capacity to intimidate voters in the camp of the opposition parties preventing them from voting. Moreover, candidates with criminal background had invariably better financial capacity of their own to splurge on illiterate and poor voters, who account for more than half of the votes in any constituency. This DNA of India, was inherited from the colonial India. Political parties have to create a new India with the DNA infused in the Preamble to the Constitution of India.

In order to have a good government that will realize the will of 'we the people of India' in experiential comforts of health, prosperity and peace at 100% population level in the earliest possible time frame, we will have to embark upon eight major action program.

1.   *The Constitution of India had laid out the objectives of Indian Republic in its Preamble. These were and are the missions of the Indian Republic expected of its every citizen to pursue in principle and practice alike. These missions were to constitute the idea of being Indians and the idea of the making of India to the citizens of the Indian Republic. The governments at the Centre and in states should make these as the missions to be achieved in fixed time frame.*

2.   *The People's Representation Act should have emphatic clause binding every political parties and their members to work for the translation of the missions of the Indian Republic into reality. Parties should be registered only when they have proven records of works having done to i) constitute India into a sovereign, socialist, secular, democratic republic; ii) to secure justice—social, economic and political; liberty of thought, expression, faith, belief and worship; equality of status and opportunity; and iii) to promote fraternity among the*

citizens assuring dignity of individual and the unity and integrity of the nation.

3. *The Election Commission of India, at present asks the parties only to declare allegiance to the Constitution of India. This is not sufficient. The Commission should look for proof of having works done to translate the 3 vital missions of the Indian Republic in concrete terms, on the part of the parties applying for registration.*

4. *Election Commission should have powers to ask every member of the political party to show proof of field work in the areas of the 3 vital missions of the Indian Republic as mandated in the Preamble to the Constitution of India. It should insist the party to give membership to only those who work among people to achieve the missions of the objectives of the Indian Republic which if implemented would translate into health, prosperity and peace at 100% population level.*

5. *The Indian Administrative Service personnel should be trained to manage the Republic of India for realizing the objectives or the Mission Statements of the Republic of India as contained in the Preamble to the Constitution of India. They should be trained as the servants of the people and not as the masters of the people, a legacy inherited from the erstwhile ICS. They should be posted at Panchayat and Municipal Wards level as development officers to create the Indian Republic as envisioned in the Preamble to the Constitution of India, from grass root level, i.e. Ward level. It is his or her duty to chalk out plans and projects for the health, prosperity and social harmony and peace of people at 100% population level. He or she should be the middle-person between the government and the people at large.*

6. *Social, economic and political justice to people can be achieved only through neighborhood schools and colleges, hospitals and nursing homes, affordable homes for all, income security for all at minimum of Rs.2 lakhs, as the GOI had already fixed as the low income in towns and cities, health for all, education for all and food for all. The Ward level IAS officers will be responsible for achieving social, economic and political justice to people. They will also be responsible for securing liberty of thought, expression, faith, belief and worship and equality of status and opportunity to people for leading happy, healthy, prosperous and peaceful lives.*

7. *The police and judicial laws and implementation procedure extant in India are not conducive to the implementation of the major mission of the Indian Republic i.e. to promote fraternity among the citizens of India ensuring their personal dignity and the unity and integrity of the communities and thereby the nation. This is because, these agencies were designed and nurtured from the times of the East India Company and later the British government which used them to control the vast Indian colony. Essentially, conceived and conditioned in a feudal atmosphere in feudal-fascist spirit, these agencies have helped only tendencies and trends opposite to fraternity in Independent India, with brutalized police force and lethargic and snail-paced justice delivery. The solution lies in framing laws suitable for a democratic republic and converting the police and judiciary into people friendly agencies capable of fraternal ways of disposing of disputes and resolve conflicts among citizens, so that most of the cases could be resolved in mutually amicable manner and only unsolved cases go to courts. No case*

should linger for more than ten months generally and in extremely special cases not more than two years, so that inter-personal and inter-groups friction and fissures caused by long pending legal tangles could be avoided.

8. *Political parties should be bound by law to give 50% of memberships to women so that half of the seats in all governments at local, state and Central levels would go to women. Equal status and equal opportunities must be conferred to women in all socio-economic activities and this can be achieved best by fixing half of all jobs in public and private sectors for women including the police and army. Government must take special care to instruct parents for giving equal status and respect to girls in homes and advise their boys to respect girls in schools and at workplaces. All political parties should share the responsibility of training their cadres for promoting equality and respect for girls across all social institutions.*

SUMMING UP

The making of India as we know it today had started when the Constitution of India was adopted by the Constituent Assembly of India on November 26, 1949. The conceptual design of the future Republic of India was enshrined in the Preamble to the Constitution of India. The detailed design of the Republic of India contained in its 395 Articles, through 22 Parts and their accompanying schedules were made in response to the objectives or the missions of the Republic of India enshrined in the Preamble to the Constitution of India.

As you might recall, in our discussion, we have maintained that the detailed design prepared by the members of the Constituent Assembly of India had not been entirely in tune with the Mission Statements of the Republic of India contained in the Preamble. Not only that, we have pointed out that some of the structuring of the government was contrary to the republican spirit of the Preamble's mandate, and that it was in line with the feudal colonial administration followed by the British government in India.

Since the British colonial government functioned in India to collect revenue to the maximum possible limit, its governance structures were tuned to that goal and when independent India's government was modeled on the pattern of those governance structures employed by British colonizers, obviously the people of India had the misfortune of having a situation in which the colonizers were driven away but their place was taken over by people of their own kind to use the structures used by the colonizers to 'crush' the people of India.

This peculiar and ridiculous situation was born because, as Jawaharlal Nehru so audaciously proclaimed in his famous book, *Discovery of India,* the 'wrong England' that came to India and ruled India in partnership with the 'wrong India,' had nurtured the 'great Indian middle class' having the DNA containing same penal and feudal codes of the nurturers. As Nehru prophetically stated in his book in 1945, this Indian middle class leaders who fought for India's independence, wanted only the British rulers to go, not their rule! Because, the rule offered enough power and pelf and the attendant glory which they themselves wanted to experience, using the same control structures shaped and strengthened by the British rulers to run their colony.

In 1946, when the British colonial government constituted the Constituent Assembly to make a Constitution for the envisioned independent India to be ruled by Indians themselves, and to form an interim government till the Constitution was framed and adopted, the members to that august body were elected on the basis of representation of religion, economic status and eminence and generally comprised people from the middle class which was the product and progeny of the feudal England and the feudal India.

The three years of Constitution making and through it, the India making or rather the Indians-making, resulted in charting out a set of noble and ideal goals for the Republic of India, as listed in the Preamble to the Constitution and a lengthy body of texts delineating the formation of a feudal-fascist-democratic society for the people to contend with. That the members of the Constituent Assembly wanted only the British people to go and not their method of rule, was amply made clear by producing the Constitution that we are having at present and by retaining the governance structures of administration, judiciary and police used by the British rulers to control us and wherever necessary to 'crush' us as was happening to us since 1950.

But the greatest tribute to Nehru's adroit judgment about Indian middle class leadership's entrenched feudalism was when Dr. Man Mohan Singh, India's Prime Minister, said in a speech at Oxford that our judiciary, our legal system, our bureaucracy and our police are all great institutions which did the country well. That Dr. Singh's speech at the Oxford University, eulogizing the British governance structure which Nehru felt was 'crushing us,' went unchallenged and un-criticized by the intelligentsia in India, proved all the more vehemently that the propensities attributed to the Indian middle class leadership by Nehru was valid even today.

We all are aware how 'great' these institutions are, aren't we? The corruption attributed to the bureaucracy is not only on bribery, but also stridently on the landlord-tenant and master-vassal relationship it has with the common people and disposal of files on public weal at its sweet will are also parts of the accusations pasted on the forehead of the Indian bureaucracy. A court case takes decades for receiving justice and police can take anyone, anytime on fabricated case and shut you up in their custody without giving a reason. These characteristics of our institutions of governance are prominent signatures of an entrenched feudal class and the self-serving behavior of this class is the root cause of India's socio-economic woes. The entire civil society is up in arms for justice from the institutions of governance which Prime Minister, Man Mohan Singh had certified as 'great institutions having served the country well.'

In the 2012 Global Hunger Index report released by the International Food Policy Research Institute in October 2012, India ranks 65th out of 79 countries. The report has sharply criticized India for not moving fast enough to reduce malnourishment, and has said that its nutritional indicators are far worse than its economic indicators. In the Human Development Index 2013, India ranked 136. In the Press Freedom Index released by Reporters Without Borders,

Washington in November, 2012, India ranked 131st, a very low index indicating how India's leadership chase away criticism about it in the Indian media, including the Internet. India's middle class is reported to be around 20 to 30% of the total population of India or around 300 million out of the total 1200 million population. The GDP of the country is mainly revolving around the middle class and the purchasing power of the rest of the population, i.e. the 900 million, is not conducive for a decent living and hence the low HDI of 136th ranking. The governance benefits go to the middle and upper class sections of the Indian society.

How feudal minded is the Indian leadership belonging to the middle class, can be gauged from the fact that more than half of Indians live in poverty while India strives to become a super power. It, is already in nuclear and space clubs.

The paradox of Indian democracy is that it follows the revenue model of government that was followed by the British rulers in India. In reality, the Republic of India's missions were for the Indian leadership to follow a development model of government. Now you know, that you cannot pluck grapes from bramble thorn bush, can you? Not in all eternity! But, a middle class born of the feudal England and the feudal India over a period of more than 300 years, was entrusted the republic of India to produce democratic development of people! Are we not still trying to gather vainly democratic fruits from the feudally entrenched ruling hierarchy belonging to the middle class?

So, my dear readers and fellow citizens, the idea of being Indians and the making of India from that idea, as of now, is not encouraging at all because, the real state of being for majority of Indians is very dismal and pathetic indeed. Since Indians are India or since Indians make India, both Indians and India in the making are dismal and pathetic.

Our way forward is to develop Indian society into a fully democratic and egalitarian republic in accordance with the Mission Statements contained in the Preamble to the Constitution of India. Constituting India into a sovereign, socialist, secular, democratic republic is our fundamental duty. Likewise, promoting justice, liberty, equality and fraternity is a fundamental duty of every citizen of this ancient nation. A 12-point good governance model titled '*sarvodaya good governance model*' has been presented before you to administer the Mission Statements of Indian Republic, as given in the Preamble to the Constitution of India. The idea of being Indians, all of us would like to cherish in our minds and then in our hearts is the healthy, prosperous and peaceful Indians at total or 100% level of the population. When a nation is at peace with itself, it can generate only universal love and peace and 'vasudhaiva kutumbakam' will be its world outlook that compels friendship and cordiality with all nations. International peace and disarmament drive will be its foreign policy.

The making of India from now on has to be the product of the idea of being Indians that we have to construct and cherish from the Mission Statements of Indian Republic enshrined in the Preamble to the Constitution of India. Let us change the feudal revenue model of governance that we follow since the days of Independence, into a republican developmental model of governance in accordance with the Mission Statements of the Indian Republic. Let us translate the *sarvodaya model of good governance* into reality in every Panchayat and Municipality Ward in India.

A democratic republican government would mean a government driven by the *sarvodaya* spirit—the spirit to serve at total or 100% population level. That is the difference between a true democratic republican government and the other forms of governments. This is what the youth of India should understand and why it should strive to infuse itself with the DNA of India, sourced in the Preamble to the Constitution of India. The making of a new India is in the hands of the youth of India. The young Indians cut across lower, middle and upper classes of Indian society and they should form a new *sarvodaya* society in India and let it show the making of the coming world on the principles of *sarvodaya*.

Let us show to the world that *Ramarajya* or the perfect governance based on the *advaita* doctrine which animated the Indian civilization through the ages is possible through the administration of *sarvodaya* good governance model. Because, the survival and salvation of human race on planet Earth to lead a happy, prosperous and peaceful life could be possible only through *sarvodaya* good governance model.